And We Call Ourselves

MEN!

Becoming The Men

We Need To Be

TRAVIS KELLY

Outskirts Press, Inc.
Denver, Colorado

Outskirts Press, Inc.
http://www.outskirtspress.com

ISBN: 978-1-4327-1160-3

Outskirts Press and the "OP" logo are trademarks belonging to Outskirts Press, Inc.

PRINTED IN THE UNITED STATES OF AMERICA

Dedication

This body of work is dedicated to Danyan Mangham, the son I never had. I think anyone who actually knows me can really understand and appreciate my desire to be a better man. In turn, it is truly my yearning to have the opportunity to play a part in the development, guidance, and influence of a being that is a part of me in some form or fashion. So to the son I never had, I dedicate this to you. And to all the sons who lack the guidance, influence, and development necessary to be a better man, I hope I've done something good!

Contents

Introduction

*W*hen I decided to take on a project of this magnitude I immediately thought about the possibility of failing in accomplishing what I'd set out to do. But after contemplating and weighing the possible outcomes I decided that failing wasn't an option for this particular endeavor. Failing isn't an option because of the impact this book may or may not have on something that I consider to be essential, us! My intent is to touch a group of individuals on a global scale. But if I fall short, if I touch only a few, then failure is only in the eye of the beholder. I've always had a desire to make a difference in anything I've chosen to do, whether it's a work-related task or the impact I make on the people I come in contact with. So it's really not a surprise to me that I didn't let a little thing like failure discourage me. If we all took the time to look in the mirror and ask ourselves: "Why am I here on this earth?" many would be hard-pressed to come up with a reasonable answer. Some *people are here on this earth to raise children, some are here to live their lives as they see fit, there are even some who are here to just take from and hurt others, and then there are some who are here to help those who can't or won't help themselves. Well, I don't know how fortunate I am but I'm one of those people who's here to help others. If I've learned anything in my lifetime I've learned this, you can only help those who want to be helped. I think it's truly a gift to have the ability to help, guide, and influence others and it's not a gift that is common among all men. But those who do have it have a responsibility that comes along with it. I'm not saying that I have that gift but I do have something to say and if what I have to say helps us to become better men and in turn better people, then what I have to say is just as great.*

I've never really considered myself to be a writer but I have been told that I can write. I've also been told that sometimes I say things I shouldn't say and it's very rare that I'm at a loss for words. So having something to say is what really inspired me to write this premise. And We Call Ourselves Men! *takes a subjective look at how we as African American men view ourselves, relationships, families, and how others view us as well. Being that the content of this manuscript is purely subjective, it is in no means a consensus of the views of African American men as a whole. Even so, the overall goal remains the same and that is to bring about change. It seems inconceivable to think that change can be brought about without some form of energy. And energy is exactly what's being brought to the table in this piece. If nothing more, this text initiates conversations that have been long overdue. It is not my intent to just initiate a conversation. The objective of* And We Call Ourselves Men! *is to become a catalyst in creating an understanding between men and women, African American men and women in particular but not exclusively. Because my affection for us is so engaging I found it difficult to take an objective approach in addressing the concerns and issues that are so hard-pressing in our society. Even though this piece is purely subjective there is no place for subjectivity when trying to create effective change if that's the overall purpose. It takes a really gifted individual to be able to form an idea inside of his or her head and make it into reality. My mother once told me that words without actions are just that, words! And I strongly believe that our words are amplified by our actions. So it is with great anticipation and desire that the words from these pages stir action.*

So when I speak of us and our plight you'll forgive me if I choose not to be pessimistic about our dilemma. It is my genuine, sincere care and concern that has brought me to this point. And with this sincere care and concern I dedicate this work to the women, daughters, wives, and mothers who are filled with disappointment, discouragement, desperation, and hopelessness. And to the men, sons, husbands, and fathers who lack understanding and are lost, confused, and ignorant, I say this: understand that we are responsible for us and the choices we make! May this piece inspire, encourage, and touch all of us in a way that is conducive to creating change. With this being said, I thank all those who are near and dear to me. If you're a part of my life or have been a part of my life in any way, shape, form, or fashion then you've inspired me in one way or another. I truly believe I'm here on this earth to help people because that's what I do best. Why are you here?

Travis Kelly
Miami, Fl
December 2008

Chapter 1
Becoming the Men We Need to Be

G rowing up without a father or a father figure isn't anything new to African American men and it's not so peculiar to a lot of Caucasian men for that matter. So what makes me and my life so different? Absolutely nothing! Unless you consider the fact that not having a father forced me to evolve into something I never expected, a man with weaknesses. These weaknesses ultimately made an impact on my development as a man, my relationships with women, and how I view the concept of fatherhood. I've always said, *It takes a person with strength and character to look at themselves and identify their own weaknesses.* It sounds a lot easier than it really is and surprisingly enough not everyone can do it, especially men. I've only recently acquired the ability to do so, and at the ripe old age of 38 it feels like a breath of fresh air after being deprived of the gift of oxygen. This may sound like it has nothing to do with becoming a man but it has everything to do with becoming a better man. Because I wasn't afforded the privilege (and yes it is a privilege) of having a father to love, guide, teach, and mold me, I've realized that for most of my young life and throughout adulthood I was always lost within myself. In a perfect world some may not consider growing up with a father a privilege but more so of an expectation. Unfortunately in the world we currently live in, growing up with a father is more of a privilege than an expectation. Some people may see this as a cliché and some may say, *What the hell does that mean?* Well, people go through life trying to find themselves every day, meaning: Who am I? What am I? Where do I come from and where am I going? These are things people spend a lifetime trying to figure out and my story is no different except I've discovered how important that missing piece was. My story is one of simplicity. You won't find any tales of fame and fortune or adventure and espionage, but what you will find is something that we can all relate to in some form or another and that's how we as young African American men evolve through a lifetime of confusion, hurt, abandonment, and resentment.

In the late 1960s my mother had just finished high school with dreams of attending a local junior college in South Florida and becoming a nurse. Little did she know that when she met my father, those dreams would all change. From her accounts he was a tall, slim dude who was fairly good-looking. They began as friends and eventually as we all know, she developed feelings. It's unclear as to whether or not the feelings were mutual but hers were the real ones—you know, the ones that don't allow you to see or hear anyone or anything else. Yeah, those were the ones. He appeared to be someone special to her as evident by her willingness to give of herself what most women consider to be the ultimate gift, her innocence. I never really valued the saying, *This child was conceived out of love* until I was able to understand what it meant for a woman to give of herself for the first time and by this I mean have her first sexual experience. She gives something she could never retrieve and that's her innocence.

Of course on the opposite side of the spectrum most young men will give their innocence away to the first willing participant (of the opposite sex, that is). If you haven't figured it out yet, I was conceived the very first time my mother gave of herself. So if I didn't value the saying *This child was conceived out of love,* I value it now more than ever before because of the circumstances in which I was conceived. After my mother realized she was pregnant my father distanced himself from her. I can only assume that the feelings she had for him weren't mutual and he wasn't ready to be the man she wanted or needed him to be. I understand that this happens every day, day in and day out all over the world, but there are different circumstances in every case. In my case I spent most of my life wondering what those circumstances were. I couldn't begin to understand those circumstances, and my mother had very few explanations and probably stopped trying to figure them out a long time ago. The only person who could begin to shed light on the negative feelings I've endured over my lifetime was the person who created them. Sometimes I wonder if he understands the ripple effect he has created and how many lives he's touched by his actions.

When my mother realized that she would be solely responsible for the guidance, influence, and care of a baby she immediately sacrificed her dreams of attending junior college and began to work at a bank to support her and myself. Initially she worked as a cashier at a local supermarket but eventually her money-handling experience landed her a job as a teller for a local bank. That's the type of woman she always was; she continuously aspired to be more than what she was and settled for nothing less than what she set her mind on. My mother has always taught and instilled in me that if you work hard you can get anything you want in life. My mother has always had a strong work ethic and taught my brother and me to be hard workers and provide for our families and ourselves. She stressed education but I'm not sure if she ever really valued anything more than a high school diploma considering that no one in my entire family had ever obtained a college degree, at least not to my knowledge. My mother has never been on public assistance and is proud to be very independent and self-maintained. As a matter of fact this may be one of her weaknesses in maintaining a viable relationship. I guess that's one more thing my father can be held responsible for. She never asked for support from my father until I was a teenager, and even then after I was almost 15 years old, he told the state of Florida that I wasn't his child. Even though I look exactly like him, he was able to deny paternity and sleep at night in good conscience. I wonder what it was like in his shoes. Being the man that I am today, I couldn't fathom what it was like in his shoes. Some people say a woman can raise a boy to be a man just as well as a man can. Well as a man raised by a woman, I can honestly say that my mother raised me to be the best human being and the best person I could be. But becoming a better man involves much more than just being a good human being or a good person for that matter.

Growing up in a culturally diverse city like Miami has

its pros and cons. One of the biggest pros is being able to learn about and learning to live with other cultures. One of the biggest cons is losing your identity within the mix of the different cultures. I didn't understand that or even recognize it until I left Miami and saw the real world. Seeing the real world means being able to see and understand the big picture. Most people find it hard to see the big picture. The big picture is larger than a small neighborhood in Miami like Liberty City, Opa Locka, Overtown, Goulds, or Perrine. The big picture consists of the way the world works (who gets what and how much) and that's something a woman could never teach me. It took a man to teach me how to deal with certain situations and certain types of individuals. While growing up in Miami I found that I was deprived of life. What I mean by life is the knowledge and understanding of how to evolve into what is considered to be the best man I could possibly be.

As I grew up in Miami I watched my mother work two jobs for most of her life so that my brother and I wouldn't only have what we needed but almost everything that we wanted. I definitely wouldn't say that we grew up with a silver spoon in our mouths but we didn't want for anything either. My mother made sure that we had decent clothes on our backs, a good roof over our heads, and more than enough to eat on the table. She did her best to shield us from the streets by moving us to a better neighborhood every chance she got. She made sure we went to the best schools in the community and even went to the school district to transfer our schools and provided our own transportation just to make sure that we had the opportunity for the best education possible. Those are just the things a mother should and would want for her children; it had nothing to do with raising a better man but it had everything to do with raising a good person. I had very few influences growing up as a boy, so the friends that I hung around swayed me heavily. Fortunately for me all my friends were into sports and girls rather than drugs and crime. They all aspired to go to college, which had an enormous impact on how I viewed attending college. I later understood that college is not something you do because all your friends are doing it. College takes a lot of dedication and determination in order to be successful at it. I had uncles but they were much older and not around much. My two uncles who were close to being young were too busy trying to figure out how to become men themselves, so they had very little time to invest in me. Luckily my mother provided me with good moral guidance, which helped me make good decisions in the friends I chose to associate with. Some people believe that you have no choice in certain situations and to some extent that's true. For example, you have no choice in what color you are when you're born or which parents you are born to. But in most or some cases your life is about choices. One of the first steps in becoming a good person and an even better man is to realize that you do have choices. Regardless of the circumstances there's going to come a time when you have a choice to make that may affect your future or the future of someone else. These very same choices are the things that help us evolve into the men we need or want to be. If these choices are guided by morals and values that reflect the world, not just Liberty City, Overtown, Opa Locka, Goulds, Perrine, or any other city or town then the likelihood of becoming a better man is highly favorable. Some people might ask, *Who determines what a better man should be?* Well, people may say a better man is determined by his reputation or people's perception of him. I would argue that a better man is determined by his ability to guide and influence others with a genuine, sincere care and concern for them. Needless to say the latter of the two is much more complex. A man's reputation is not as important as the legacy he leaves behind. Of course some people would be inclined to disagree with this point of view but if you entertain the possibility that a man with the ability to guide and influence others with a genuine, sincere care and concern for them and can apply it across the political, social, and economic spectrum, then he would encompass the very essence of manhood (theoretically). You see, the essence of manhood does not only consist of how you perceive yourself but also how others perceive you as well. If you look at any man who you consider to be good in nature or character, there is an air about him that makes people feel at ease and comfortable. There's also an air of confidence and security in the way he presents himself. He's aware of who he is and what he needs to be in order to make everything right. When a woman looks to a man, a child looks to a father, a sister to a brother, and a mother looks to a son, they're all looking for him to make things right when things are wrong. And as men we are obligated to make sure we understand that it is our responsibility, our duty, our place in this world and in life to make whatever is wrong feel right again. When a young man evolves into the man he is meant to be, then and only then will he be looked at as what is considered to be a better man. This process doesn't happen overnight and it doesn't happen in your own backyard. Becoming a better man is a constant job; it takes a conscious effort to make yourself better day in and day out. And when you think you've done it all, do more! I know, I know, it sounds easier said than done but it's very easy to not have a care or concern about anyone or anything except yourself. It takes a different kind of man to make a conscious decision to try and do the right thing day in and day out, and notice I used the word "try." It's imperative that men understand we are just that, men! We are not perfect and those who strive to be do fall short from time to time. We should consider our shortcomings to be a way of life. With all of our weaknesses, faults, and failures, our goal remains the same and that is to be the best men we can possibly be.

I left Miami and joined the military in order to develop discipline, maturity, and growth, and it's probably the best thing that could have happened to me as a young man. Please don't take this statement out of context; I'm not saying that all young African American men should join the military. What I am saying is that it was the best option for me at that time. By the time I was 20 years old I had flunked out of two colleges and had never read a book. What I'm saying is, I had never read a book from cover to cover. You would think that while in public school for 13 years I would have read at least one book. I'm sure there are thousands of young African American men who could say the same. What prompted me to read a book was an incident that occurred while I was stationed overseas in Europe while in the United States Air Force. Being new to the base I wasn't real careful about who I chose to hang out with. Usually if a person is from the same geographical area or even region you tend to have something in common so you hang out a little bit. One night I was hanging out with some dudes from the South and by the South I mean South Carolina, Georgia, Alabama, etc... We decided to hang out at the NCO Club on the base one Saturday night. I had probably been on the base for about two weeks. As we walked into the club we went straight to the bathroom because we had been drinking Bacardi 151 Rum in my room prior to going to the club. As we went into the bathroom we must have walked past a group of women because as we came out of the bathroom one of the women accused me of grabbing her from behind. The woman was a young to middle-aged white female with a behind like a surfboard (long and flat), so because of my lack of curiosity for white women, I had no interest in touching her in any kind of way, and besides, being where I'm from women get grabbed in the club all the time. So I politely blew her off and continued on my way through the club. Shortly thereafter, as I stood at the bar I noticed the same group of women walking towards me with a law enforcement officer in tow. I thought, *You've got to be kidding me.* The chick with the surfboard backside pointed me out as the guy who grabbed her. I was immediately arrested for battery and processed at the Law Enforcement Station on the base. My first sergeant arrived and I was released pending an investigation. I was several thousand miles away from home with no guidance, no support, and without anyone to advise me of what was going on. The mother who raised me couldn't teach me how to deal with the world as it was for me at that time and I strongly believe that only a man could have. Only a man, only an African American man for that matter, could have taught me how to deal with and understand the role that we as African American men play within a predominately white society. Two weeks later I stood at attention as my squadron commander reprimanded me. He asked me how I would like it if someone grabbed my black girlfriend's behind! The question threw me for a loop; I mean I was literally perplexed. Once he uttered those words everything else became irrelevant. All I could think about was, where did the black and white issue come in? That particular incident influenced me to read my first book. I went to the base library and I got books on criminal justice, law enforcement, constitutional law, and criminal procedure. I wanted to know everything I needed to know in order to defend myself. I wanted to know what rights were afforded to me and what particular consequences I may face. As a matter of fact, I learned so much from those books that I was able to CLEP my way through three college courses. Unfortunately it took an incident like that, which occurred in a matter of minutes and thousands of miles away from home in a place that was totally unfamiliar to me, for me to read a book from cover to cover for the first time. That one incident accomplished what my mother and several teachers couldn't accomplish in a matter of 13 years.

I truly believe that the military plays a part in teaching young men how to be better men, but that's not necessarily true of all men. And by that I mean the military exposes men to life experiences that a father can only tell his son about. I guess that's why young African American men who are deprived of the guidance of a father figure struggle with transitioning into the military way of life. Oftentimes the military makes you live in a place you don't want to live, do a job you don't want to do, and live with people you don't want to live with. How much better can a young man be prepared for the world than that? I mentioned that story because at that point in my life no one had taken responsibility for making me a better man. *And we call ourselves men!* How can we call ourselves men when we refuse to take responsibility for us? If it wasn't apparent to me then, it is now. If we don't take responsibility for us and ours, meaning our lives, our relationships and our children, then who will? There were several older African American airmen and sergeants in my squadron who knew exactly what was happening to me and none of them bothered to take responsibility for me by guiding me in the right direction or even supporting me by giving me advice. It kind of felt like I was on a plantation and while getting in trouble with the master the other slaves watched and did nothing out of fear. In attempting to become better men and ultimately the men we need to be, we have to be able to take responsibility for us. Because of the big picture we as African American men are obligated to take responsibility for ourselves. A lot of times as young men we tend to get caught up in our own sense of being, which is just a small part of the big picture. Life consists of more than just our own self-fulfilling needs and wants. I'm not saying our own needs and wants aren't important, but if we look at life as it's really intended to be then we'll come to understand that the way we touch those with whom we come in contact can directly impact the way we are perceived. In that aspect, being a better man may consist of more than just how smart you are or how well you treat your woman or your kids, but it also consists of what kind of impact you make on those with whom you come in contact, from the stranger on the bus to the people at work as well as the brother and sister at church. And when I say impact I don't mean entertaining someone or making them laugh. I mean touching them in a way that changes the way they look at themselves and others. In our lifetime we can name several good men who sacrificed their own personal welfare for the good of others. But the sacrifice that is necessary for change has to come on a wider scale. Putting others before yourself may seem to be too much to ask, but if we all made the same sacrifice then it wouldn't be unachievable and not too much to expect. Not to mention that if we all made the same sacrifice then it wouldn't seem so unattainable. It's understood that we are all human, and selfishness is a human characteristic but sacrificing doesn't necessarily mean always putting others before your self. We unknowingly make sacrifices every day that affect others. This concept isn't something we're born with; it has to be taught and modeled and it starts with us!

What I've learned in life is this: young boys look for role models to emulate, young girls look for models to admire, and women look for men to respect. It's up to us to decide what type of role models we present to them. It starts here! We have to work on ourselves before we can be a role model for any woman or child whether it's a girl or a boy. We have to transform ourselves and the way we think before we can expect to make an impact on the women we seek and the children we raise. Where do we start? Well, what do we value? Society says that we value luxury cars, jewelry, and clothes. If this statement is true then I would argue that these values are not necessarily a bad thing but what is bad are the things we are willing to sacrifice for them. There's nothing wrong with having a nice car, nice clothes, or nice things, but what sacrifice are they worth? Are they worth being in so much debt that you're working just to pay creditors? Are they worth being incarcerated for? Are they worth possibly taking someone's life for or even having your life taken? Even though these values are not necessarily bad, they definitely shouldn't be a priority. If nice things aren't the priority then what is? There are certain things that are necessary in order to set a foundation for achieving certain goals in life. A lot of times we tend to look for shortcuts in order to meet the goals we set, whether they are short-term or long-term goals. The things we sacrifice are indicative of the shortcuts we take in life. For example, living outside of our means is a sacrifice we make in contrast to budgeting our resources and practicing patience for the things we desire. It's not uncommon to us and we've all done it at some time or another and in some cases it's a common practice. A formal education is a value that is not considered to be a priority by many, and in some cases having a formal education is not necessarily a prerequisite for success. But what a formal versus an informal education does is open the door for opportunities that may not have been available otherwise. These opportunities are what comprise some of the first steps in evolving into what we need to be as better men. Unfortunately when these opportunities are presented to us we've had a history of not taking advantage of the possibility of establishing a foundation for success in achieving certain life goals such as the nice things I mentioned before. A lot of times this is because we fail to make the correlation between education and success. Establishing a foundation in which to work is one of the first steps in developing the qualities of a good person, a good human being, and ultimately a better man. Regrettably we've seen the foundation set by images that portray behaviors that are contrary to the concept of becoming a better man. All too often have we seen the images of hustling and taking shortcuts to get what we want or need in life versus working hard and earning everything we get or need. The differences between the two are: there are consequences to one and rewards to the other. It's admirable for a woman and a child to see her man and their father get up and go to work every day and expect him to come home and make everything right. Surprisingly enough this admiration has its limits. We tend not to see the reward in doing what's right because we look for immediate gratification without considering the long term or the big picture. I don't know if being able to see the big picture or the long term comes with maturity or if it's something that can be instilled at an early period. But not understanding the relevance of it is detrimental to the growth and development of us as better men. It's amazing how we have a false sense of reality when it comes to the real world and what role we play in it. We have a tendency to look at life from a skewed perspective. Our values, ideals, and morals are shaped by a very small piece of the big picture and it places us at a disadvantage, from our education to the way we view our women, our children, our families, and our community as a whole. Sometimes we just don't get it! We just don't understand how significant our role is in the accomplishments of us.

A foundation is set through vision. As I said before, it takes a gifted individual to envision something in his or her head and make it into reality. This gift is not common but it is a gift nevertheless and can be passed on from person to person and generation to generation. My philosophy of life starts with what I call the 40/40 theory. The 40/40 theory is not some big complex hypothesis. Actually it's quite simple in nature and applies to all men across all races, ethnicities, and cultures. Generally we consider the age 40 to be middle-aged. Some may beg to differ but for argument's sake let's say 80 years old is the typical life expectancy for a man, any man of any race or culture. If 80 is the typical life expectancy then 40 is middle-aged. The theory is this: most men either spend their first 40 years having fun, doing their own thing, or just finding themselves as they say, while others spend their first 40 establishing a family and raising children. For some it's the exact opposite—they spend their first 40 years establishing a family and raising children while utilizing the next 40 years to have fun, do their own thing, or just find themselves. There is nothing wrong with taking either of these approaches to life as long as we understand that there are pros and cons that come along with each. Some may even argue that you can establish a family, raise children, have fun, do your own thing, and find yourself all at once. This concept is much more intricate and raises several dilemmas when addressing conflicts of interest and priorities. This concept brings into question which is the priority—the family, the children, having fun, doing your own thing, or finding yourself? Usually if you choose one concept versus the other the chances of being successful at it is less likely than not. So as we set the foundation for becoming better men we should understand what we value versus what we should value. Once we understand what we should value and what our values really are, then establishing the foundation for becoming a better man will be essential. If the goal is to inspire and encourage a magnitude of individuals, there is no room for prerequisites. But as we aspire to inspire those of us who are remiss in being better, we should understand that we don't have to be a certain age or come from a certain class or educational background. What's needed is a willingness, some ambition, a sense of obligation, and a little motivation to be better than what we are. So 40 years old is not too old and 16 years old is not too young. Many times while attempting to establish a foundation we tend to allow others or external influences to dictate who we are as men. Becoming a better man means establishing who you are without letting anyone or anything dictate who you are or what you develop to be. Keep in mind that this also entails establishing a foundation to evolve from.

There is one thing I don't think many of us understand and that's how our peer associations influence the type of men we become. It's a reasonable assumption to think that if you surround yourself with certain individuals with positive influences, then you will assimilate their morals and values. This can also be assumed in surrounding yourself with others of a negative influence. Now this is not necessarily true for all individuals but for the most part one could agree. These types of peer associations can be seen from our teenage years throughout adulthood. Our peers play a major part in how we view certain situations at times. The same could be said for our female counterparts. This is especially evident in dealing with a dilemma. If we choose to associate with individuals who have less than our best interest at heart then we tend to put ourselves in situations that are damaging to our own well-being. This is why it is so important to recognize that a man's character should be judged by how well he handles adversity and how resilient he is because as the teacher, provider, protector, and head of household it's vital for him to be able to stand up and lead his family and children when there is confusion and a lack of direction. It is also important to acknowledge the fact that every man, especially African American men, may not have the ability to handle adversity and have resiliency, but we must all realize and would agree that without these attributes, attaining the objective of becoming a better man can be futile. When we think about all the adversity we encounter on a day-to-day basis, just being able to function is a task in itself. In today's society just waking up and going to a job that barely pays your bills is discouraging enough. But when we think about other aspects of life that we consider essential, adversity should be considered a way of life. For some of us it's as simple as getting up and going to work, but for others coping with the day-to-day stressors of life can be overwhelming. These stressors are magnified for African American men and it's unfortunate that our families inherit these same stressors. So it's our responsibility to ensure that the stressors we face don't become obstacles or barriers for those we're responsible for. We can't continue to allow our women and our children to become the ill-fated beneficiaries of the same adversity we strive to overcome daily. Just as it is our responsibility to shield them from harm and despair it is equally our responsibility to create and provide opportunities for them. The reality is that we're all we have and our women and children need us. As we look at ourselves and determine our own fate, we should always consider the big picture and what part we as African American men play in it. Understanding our plight enables us to better prepare for our evolution as men, husbands, and fathers. Understanding our plight means understanding that we can't use racism as a justification for not having integrity. Understanding our plight means we can't allow our environment to dictate who we are but that we decide what type of men we evolve into. Understanding our plight means understanding that we have a choice in deciding our fate. Understanding our plight means understanding that as husbands, fathers, and men we're responsible for the lives entrusted to us, not Section-8 housing, not public assistance, and certainly not child support enforcement. Conspiracy theories of how the government plans to keep African American men oppressed and incarcerated do nothing to help our predicament. It's futile for us to sit back and demand that we be paid for something that is not acknowledged as being owed. In other words, America owes us nothing! This is the type of mentality we must have in order to surmount our own self-defeating beliefs. I can imagine that many will disagree with this idea but I've seen all too many of us use what America allegedly owes us as an excuse or a justification for a lack of responsibility or accountability for our own selves, relationships, and children. Instead of squandering our time and effort on theories that don't address our primary issues we should dedicate our efforts to accurately identifying these issues and producing viable solutions to resolve them. Generally speaking, the reality is that if we didn't take other people's things, rob, steal, sell drugs, and commit crimes, we wouldn't be incarcerated. And I know there are those who may say the conditions in which we live give us no choice in the things we do to survive. Well, I would maintain the exact opposite. We do have choices! But when we choose to sacrifice our pride and dignity for a shortcut instead of earning what we get through gainful employment and hard work then we have to take responsibility and accept accountability for those choices. And not only that! If we didn't use drugs we wouldn't be oblivious to the cares and concerns of our women and children. It's amusing how we always find it simpler for us to identify the solutions rather than recognize the problem. Identifying ineffective solutions is not as vital as pinpointing the actual problem. The problem is; we've made several excuses as to our lack of progress in closing the disparity of the disproportionate amount of political, social, economic, and educational opportunities afforded to us. Other communities value not only post secondary education but they also value general educational opportunities as well, while we tend to focus on things that are superficial. I find it hard to place blame on others for our own lack of priority and focus. One of the reasons I mentioned education is because education is the single most critical factor that enables us to be successful in life. Not knowing or understanding what others understand and know is a disadvantage. When we're placed at a disadvantage it makes us vulnerable or susceptible to manipulation and exploitation. I often find that individuals who choose not to attend college usually find it offensive or tend to become defensive when there is emphasis placed on higher education. We shouldn't feel threatened by education, the relevance of it, or someone else's desire to obtain it. It should always be our intent to encourage and not to discourage any kind of interest in the advancement of us. Like I said before, it's very easy to not have a single care or concern for anyone or anything else other than yourself. What is difficult is having a genuine, sincere care and concern for others while making an honest effort to do the right thing day in and day out. So when we talk about us, let's talk about taking responsibility for us and not how others are conspiring to dictate who we are or what we will be. Let's initiate the conversations that identify our flaws and weaknesses. And once we've done that, let's initiate the conversations that address those flaws and how we can strengthen those weaknesses. Even more so, let's extend the hand that's necessary to help guide and influence others who are less cognizant of what we should be not only as men but as better men.

Change does not occur through dialogue alone. After we've initiated all of these conversations, action must take place, and it starts with us as individuals. As was stated previously, words without actions are just that, words! That's how we become better men and that's how we take responsibility for us. That doesn't mean taking to the streets and blaming others for our inability to do what not only is right by our own women and children but what is right under the law of the land. I understand that there are different circumstances in some cases, but how long can we allow circumstances to be the crutch on which we lean? I don't know how others view the word circumstance but in many ways circumstances can be synonymous with excuses and if this is so, then circumstances are things people use to cover up the truth. It is truly disheartening to hear how we place blame on others. Granted there are situations in which blame must be placed on others. I'm not saying that society is totally innocent in contributing to the lack of success for

African American men. Of course there are concerns that should and need to be addressed. When we look at the systematic disenfranchisement of the African American community through deliberate targeting of certain urban demographics in areas such as entertainment, business, education, and housing, the blame should be placed rightfully with its owner. And when we discuss the disproportionate amount of African American men who are treated unequally in opportunities that they are clearly suitable for, the unequal treatment of African Americans in the justice system, discriminatory practices of commercial businesses, and blatant disrespect, then those are the external factors beyond our control that limit our choices. These disparities which we only share with our women and not our Caucasian counterparts and some other minorities for that matter, is where our attention should be focused. But accurately identifying our issues must come first in order for us to be able to resolve them and create our own revolution. Oops! Did I say revolution? I meant evolution. Not to sound corny but I guess you could say we must be able to resolve in order to evolve.

As frustration sets in and hopelessness begins to consume us we are apt to develop features that are uncommon to us as men. We can all agree that men and women are different in many ways and in some ways we share things in common. There are certain traits that are prevalent in women and shouldn't be found in the character of men. I know we're all human and some would disagree with this point of view but character traits such as jealousy, envy, vindictiveness, and spitefulness are all human traits but are predominately found in women. I'm not saying that men can't possess any or even all of these traits, nor am I saying that all men do. What I'm saying is that these traits should not be common among men in general. These traits are arguably driven by emotions and as we'll discuss later, women are very emotional and insecure. Therefore, when men display these particular traits it's usually indicative of a lack of control of their emotions. Now I'm not speaking of physical jealousy or envy. I'm discussing the type of jealousy, envy, vindictiveness, and spitefulness that is created from the natural insecurities all women share. Things like the way another person looks, carries themselves, or even the attention they receive are all examples of how those types of traits originate in women and shouldn't be generally found in men. When these types of traits are found in men they create divisiveness in our efforts in taking responsibility for us. This has become even more disturbing in how we struggle among each other.

It is common in our day-to-day lives to have to establish a position so that we are looked upon as men of intellect, morals, values, strength, and leadership. It is even more troubling when we all have the same goal in common but because of envy, discontent, dislike, disrespect, and flat-out jealousy for each other, we tend to tear away at the very foundation we try time and time again to create. Not only do we have to be concerned with the obstacles that others place in our path, we also have to worry about the barriers we create for ourselves. This has been an issue of concern for us for as long as we could take into account. Sometimes we can be our own worst adversary. The ignorance we encounter sometimes is truly amazing. In fact, it can be downright puzzling at times. And when I say ignorance I mean not knowing. The images we portray, the decisions we make, and the perceptions we create all have negative connotations attached to them. We tend to use our culture as a justification for the things we do and say. But at some point and time we have to realize that our culture is not the only culture within our society. It's important that we understand that there is a big world outside of our own existence and if we strive to be better men then we have to be able to adapt to certain situations once they arise. We can't resolve issues at work or in public the same way we resolve them at home. We can't settle disputes and disagreements in public the way we settle them in our households. Street credibility is irrelevant once the accountability for that credibility is thrust upon you. The regrets and remorse become of no importance. The expectations of empathy and compassion turn into excuses for the ignorance we exhibit. We can't continue to blame the ignorance we display on our circumstances and situations. If we don't take ourselves seriously, how can we expect others to? We pick and choose when we want to be taken seriously, and when we're not taken seriously, we have the audacity to feel disrespected. *And we call ourselves men!* How can we consider ourselves leaders, protectors, teachers, providers, and heads of households when we can't revolutionize the way others see us or even how we see ourselves?

As we look at the big picture there are very few who are able to succeed on their own terms. Success on your own terms is very rare and is not the norm, especially for African American men. Those who are successful on their own terms should be considered the exception and shouldn't be looked upon as the blueprint for success. For those of us who aren't as fortunate, success is usually achieved on someone else's terms. As African American men we often feel that if we integrate into mainstream American society, we have to give up our identity as African Americans. This perception can't be further from the truth. If being successful means in doing so we must integrate into mainstream society then as better men conflicts of interest should be nonexistent. We all know and understand that we as African Americans are minorities within the continent in which we live. Therefore it is inevitable that if we intend on being successful at achieving our desired objectives, then adapting or integrating into mainstream society is a necessity. Regardless of what we want to believe, the reality is that we don't live in a separate society. Our ethnic cultures may be divided but society as a whole is not separate. We have to be able to succeed within the terms that society as a whole dictates, not those of our own inclination.

I understand that there are some who may have achieved success on their own terms but as previously stated those individuals are the exception to the rule. We should understand that being successful in being better men and accomplishing our objectives involves more than just our own self-fulfilling needs and wants. The needs and wants of others should be considered as well. So as we refuse to integrate into the melting pot that is considered mainstream society we should consider the consequences that not only affect us as better men but the women, children, and families we're obligated to. When we refuse to groom ourselves neatly, stop using illegal drugs, and develop employability skills in order to obtain and retain the ability to provide for ourselves and our families through gainful employment, we're attempting to resist or reject the terms that society as a whole has placed on success. While we attempt to address the issues that press our community and our society as a whole the primary focus should consist of taking ownership of the role we play in our own lack of progression. It's easy to point the finger and place blame somewhere other than at our own conscience. There comes a time in every man's life and particularly in our lives as African American men when we have to take responsibility and accept accountability for the decisions we make, not only as husbands and fathers but as better men in general. There are several opportunities that have been afforded to us and yet time and time again we've failed to take advantage of them. For example, how many of us as African Americans have thought about or wanted to attend college but weren't financially able? We all know that the government offers assistance to individuals who want to attend college through grants or even loans. How many of us have accepted government grants but have failed to put forth as much effort in studying, reading, and learning as we do in going to the club, concerts, and other events? Eventually this kind of behavior leads to failure in maintaining the required grade point average or obtaining a satisfactory grade in the course in order to retain the government grant.

Another example of how we don't utilize the opportunities that are afforded to us is the award of athletic scholarships. When we don't utilize athletic scholarships for their intended purpose we fall short of taking full advantage of that opportunity. The primary purpose of those opportunities should be foremost, which is to obtain a formal education that will create opportunities that would not have existed otherwise. These are just a couple of examples that I'm sure we can all relate to in some form or fashion, whether we've experienced them personally or we've been acquainted or are acquainted with someone who has. These opportunities are not just available to African Americans alone; they're available to most or all individuals of a lower socioeconomic status. Yet and still we have the unmitigated gall to be upset or disgruntled when individuals from other countries but of the same economic status take advantage of those same opportunities. Where does the blame lie? When do we take responsibility for us? We can't continue to allow those types of issues to be barriers to our advancement as better men. In order to be better there has to be a want or need to do so. Some would argue that we as African American men don't lack the want or need to be better but that we lack the ability to ask for and receive help in being better. Quite frankly the entire notion of individuals lacking the ability to receive help at being better men is absurd, unless there is a physical or mental impairment that obstructs an individual's ability to comprehend the basic social skills such as conflict resolution, work ethics, pro-social values, verbal and nonverbal communication, etc. This argument would suggest that we as African Americans and African American men in particular are inferior to those who have the ability to be better men. In other words, to suggest that we don't know how to ask for and receive help is as ludicrous as saying we're second best to others. We know how to ask for and receive help from the financial aid offices of the world, we know how to ask for and receive help from the Section-8 housing and public assistance offices of the world, and we know how to ask for and receive help from those who have less than our best interest at heart. In some cases many consider these gestures as some sort of rites of passage or entitlement. So to imply that we don't know how to ask for and receive help from each other in being better men is ridiculous in theory and is asinine in reality. Life is about choices; we have a choice in the decisions we make, good, bad, or indifferent! But as I digress, the one thing we should understand is that no one is going to treat us special because we are African

American and to expect such a thing is a false sense of reality.

As preparation is a necessity for success we can't expect to achieve success without preparing for it first. Preparation is necessary for any kind of success, whether it is something as simple as completing an employment application or completing a college degree. Oftentimes we're ill-prepared for not only our personal goals or aspirations but for life in general. Taking responsibility for us involves taking responsibility for our preparation as better men as well. As we prepare to take responsibility for us there has to be an understanding of how our previous patterns of having a lack of responsibility for us has affected our goals and aspirations. We have to be able to transform the way we think in order to change the desired outcomes. I know a lot of times this is a lot easier said than done. But in making us better men we have to be able to identify the factors that contribute to our lack of responsibility for us. One of the most admirable characteristic of a better man is his ability to accept responsibility for not necessarily the choices that he makes but for those choices that affect someone other than himself. In this we have to be able to take responsibility for the choices we've made that have affected others such as our women, children, and family in general. As better men this becomes a part of our legacy. As we're able to recognize our ability to take responsibility not only for our choices but how they affect others, we have to be able to understand what influences these choices have on the desired outcome. So the case that I would make is that there is not necessarily a lack of opportunities; rather we lack preparation in making choices that are conducive to being successful in becoming better men. Many so-called African American intellectuals would argue that this is a systematic result of slavery and the oppression of

African Americans that has re-emerged from the past. I would contend that theories such as these do nothing more than perpetuate the stereotype that we as African Americans continuously make excuses for our own shortcomings instead of taking responsibility for our own misgivings. Just as we can't continue to use slavery as a justification for our flaws as men, we can't allow others to dictate our place as it pertains to the big picture. I'm not saying that we don't have obstacles to hurdle as they relate to the state of African Americans and our country as whole. To put it in simpler terms, what I am saying is that we have to be able to circumvent those obstacles in order to achieve our objectives.

It's always been a trait or characteristic of our culture to be divisive among each other. And once again, many so-called intellectuals would attribute this to the effects of the peculiar institution of slavery and some would say that it is an intentional ploy by others to confine us to a state of oppression. Unfortunately the result of this divisiveness is the cause of our own inability to collaborate and attain our overall intent that should be and is beneficial to all of us, not just a select few. As we reflect upon our past, ponder the present, and anticipate our future, the idea of being a better man should be profoundly intoxicating to us. The concept alone is thought-provoking in itself. But for those of us who have grown complacent with the conditions in which we currently exist, we have yet to reach the pinnacle of our efforts in making us better. And yet we fail to comprehend how our inability to unify derails the process as we strive to move forward as better men. As evident in our current state we find division not only among our better men but also among the best of our men. In several instances we lack discretion in our efforts to attempt to guide and influence others. When we undermine our peers and colleagues, our ability to be genuine and sincere comes into question. The better man strives to exemplify sincerity and is the personification of integrity. So as we make our own individual efforts to become and influence better men it is understood that the divisiveness we face is inevitable but the better man will always be the individual who is able to guide and influence others with a genuine, sincere care and concern for them. Addressing these types of issues is what it will take to make the initial step in moving towards what we strive to achieve. Becoming a better man is more than just a physical maturation; it's a spiritual growth that transcends a physical sense. Becoming a better man encompasses the development of the mind, body, and our very own soul. So when we talk about becoming better men let's be sure we understand what it truly entails. It means sacrificing by doing things you don't want to do for the overall good of others. It means being an example for those to admire and emulate. It means separating yourself from those who strive to be less than what they are. Many men may claim to be a good man or even a better man, but self-proclamation does not make it so. Actually, self-proclamation does nothing more than display an inflated self-image, which is indicative of conceit and self-centeredness. Better men are recognized by others and are not self-proclaimed. Individuals who are compelled to exclaim to be better men are usually insincere and lack humility. There are often times when we tend to confuse confidence with arrogance. Not to say that arrogance is necessarily a bad thing but it is often confused with conceit and overconfidence. As better men we should be careful of giving the perception of overconfidence. Notice I said overconfidence and not confidence alone. There is definitely nothing wrong with being confident. As a matter of fact, as men it is expected that we display some degree of confidence. So as better men why should it not be expected that we exhibit a certain degree of more confidence? If it's our place to lead and be the head of our households there has to be an air of confidence about ourselves in our ability to do so. Not only that, confidence is one of the most important traits we lack during one of the most critical points in our development as not only better men but as men in general.

So what are we willing to do to become better men? This question can only be answered by us. It can't be answered by the Republicans. It can't be answered by the Democrats. It can't be answered by a judge or a jury. And it definitely can't be answered by our Caucasian counterparts! Speaking of our Caucasian counterparts, I find it ironic that as we discuss our issues and how we're responsible for us that one of the biggest impacts that has been made on my life came from one of our Caucasian counterparts. It was a professor at the University of Maryland (European Division) who defined the ideology of politics for me. He explained that politics is the ideology of *who gets what and how much.* It sounded simple enough at the time but when I thought about it, it was one of the most profound statements that I had heard at that age. You see, if politics is the ideology of who gets what and how much, then if we play a part in politics, we'll play a part in who gets what and how much. So if we look at politics as it's meant to be, then we would understand that politics plays a part in our everyday lives no matter how large or how small. Realizing how having some kind of influence as to who gets certain opportunities, how many opportunities, and what kind of opportunities gives us insight into the role we play in the big picture. This ideology becomes very useful when seeking opportunities that are necessary in order to achieve certain goals in life. Learning about how the world works is something I don't think my mother or any other woman could have taught me. I believe only a man could have made me understand how the world works in this aspect, preferably a black man for that matter. And I say that only because I believe our dilemma is different from others and depending upon the perception in which it's observed, this concept can often be skewed by a different perspective. Once I learned the ideology of politics my life experiences helped me apply it to the predicament of African Americans and African American men in particular. Politics involves more than just politicians, government, and what you read about or see and hear on television; politics involves your career, your relationships, your family, and your community as a whole. There is one issue that I don't believe we comprehend and that is that politics is not necessarily black and white. If you take a look at the big picture, politics is not necessarily based on race. Some would like to believe that politics is driven by race but when we discuss politics we have to be careful that we don't lose sight of the big picture.

The big picture is not based on color. So we as African American men should realize that our role is not essentially based on the color of our skin. Some may beg to differ but I would make the same argument that has been one of the tenets of the civil rights movement, and that is, *we should all be judged by the content of our character and not by the color of our skin.* And by this I mean we all should judge and support our leaders, our men, and role models by the content of their character and not just by the color of their skin simply because they're African American. We as African Americans tend to be more forgiving of our own as opposed to being forgiving of others. It has always puzzled me as to why. Does the mere fact of African American ancestry entitle us to unconditional forgiveness? Many may not be inclined to agree with me but just as we strive and set expectations to be better men, we should also set the same standards for those we consider to be our leaders. So as better men let's not just put our support and faith in those who claim to have our best interest at heart just because they're of African American descent. Our expectations should be higher and the accountability should be greater simply because we should expect that our leaders would have a vested interest in our plight and our achievements in particular as opposed to someone who is not of African American descent. So as we consider our plight as African American men and the role we play in the big picture, we should understand how vital it is that we understand the concept of politics and how it influences not only ourselves but our relationships, our family, and our community as a whole. Understanding how *who gets what and how much* is critical for us, not only as men but particularly for us as African American men because of the disparity in opportunities that are afforded to us. This idea is most relevant because of the impact it plays on not only ourselves but our relationships and our families as well. You see, becoming a better man has nothing to do with self-preservation. Becoming a better man has to do with making an impact on others by creating a transformation, an evolution, a difference. These are the principles that better men adhere to regardless of how small or how large; the objective is to produce something good and better.

Chapter 2
Relationships, Love, and Consequences

U nfortunately, with love comes consequences and that's not necessarily a bad thing. Relationships are hard work and it's important to understand that before entering into them lightly. What's really important in understanding relationships is that they're living entities. A relationship evolves, grows, develops, and changes with time. Individuals grow closer together and further apart every day and that's why relationships are considered to be hard work. After putting in an eight- to ten-hour workday at your place of employment you should expect to come home and put in another eight to ten hours of work towards your relationship and hopefully you might get four to eight hours of sleep (eight hours if you're one of the lucky ones). Not only are relationships hard work but they are also considered to be an investment. Men as well as women invest in relationships with hopes of receiving a return for their investment. Things such as time, attention, emotions, effort, and even money are all considered resources that are invested into relationships, and when there are resources invested into anything, the expectation is that you'll receive something in return. Hence the saying, *You'll only get out of it what you put in it.*

Now, what is actually received may vary depending on your objective in seeking the relationship in the first place. For those of us who are less studious the objective may be physical gratification or sex. For others the objective may be long term or maybe even marriage. Whatever the objective is the expectation is the same and that is to receive a return on the investment. Just like any other investment there are risks involved and that's what make relationships so unattractive. I think that's why relationships don't appeal to a lot of African American men. It's only natural to assume that with relationships come responsibilities and once again it goes back to us taking responsibility for us and our relationships as well. I don't think I've had problems in desiring a meaningful relationship; I just haven't been able to sustain one. At age 38 I'm still single with no children and currently not in a relationship. I have personal aspirations of being in a relationship but I do find it ironic that a man such as myself is having a difficult time in establishing a meaningful relationship. If statistics say that there are at least three African American women for every one African American man, and with almost a million African American men being imprisoned, you would think that I would be able to find one, just one! I don't even want the three that statistics say I should have, I just want one. It's really strange how life repeats itself. The first time I had sex I was 15 years old and she was 14. I broke her heart because once we had sex I thought I had to stop seeing her in order to have sex with other girls. I don't know if most men have a conscience about that sort of thing but I remember it at age 38 like it happened yesterday. She was really hurt; she cried and cried and couldn't understand why I didn't want to be with her anymore. I told her that she had changed when in reality it was I who had changed. When I think about it, it's probably how my father felt about my mother but that's no excuse for his lack of responsibility for me. At 15 years old I didn't understand the ramifications of my actions and there wasn't anyone around to show me what it meant to her and what it should've meant to me. I didn't understand the ripple effect it would have on her. I'm sure I played a part in how she felt about herself, her self-worth, and how she perceived men at that time. As I got older I realized what kind of damage I may have caused and I later apologized but of course it didn't mean much to her after the fact. The experience alone made me a better man. I learned to empathize with how she must have felt and that played a part in how I handled relationships with other women. I made a conscious decision to treat women with respect and I mean all women, regardless of how they treat themselves. I generally love all women: short, tall, skinny, or fat, and I treat them as such. When I say I love all women it's not meant to be taken in the physical sense. I have a genuine, sincere care and concern for them and I guess that's what makes me different from a lot of my peers. I'm not saying that I'm the only man in the world with this quality but I do try to make an honest effort to be the man I need to be and understand that all I can do is make an honest effort. In all good conscience I try to do the right thing by women. Now does that mean I always accomplish that goal? No! Hell no! But every day I awake I try to be a little better than I was the day before and if I accomplish those little things day in and day out, then I've made myself a better man.

Even so, it's very difficult to respect a woman who doesn't respect herself. These types of women are usually easily manipulated and are often exploited. In some ways it's human nature to prey on other's weaknesses. Be that as it may, being better men means standing out from the rest of the group. If we were all better men, then the premise of this book would be ineffectual. Standing aside from the crowd means being unlike others and being a better man definitely means standing aside from the rest. With this being said, as better men we must be able to respect all women regardless of whether or not they respect themselves. What makes us better men is how we compare and contrast to our peers. So if one of our attributes is a common respect for all women regardless of how much they respect themselves, then we've created a degree of separation from our peers. The things we do, the things we say are all indicative of the amount of respect we have for our women from our mothers, sisters, and partners to our daughters. Our actions speak volumes of our desire to be better than what's expected of us.

As far as relationships are concerned I've found that our women have been deprived of what they're rightfully entitled to and that's a relationship that puts them foremost. When I say "our women" I mean African American women because I don't date outside of my race and I'm not saying that I haven't because I have. Being in the military and being from Miami I've been with Caucasian women and dated women of Cuban and Haitian descent. The cultural differences were too much for me to adapt to. They really wanted to hold on to their culture and I really wasn't willing to give mine up, so it never really worked out too well. When I say I've been with Caucasian women I mean I've had a physical relationship with four or five while I was in the military stationed overseas. It wasn't by preference—in Europe on the military bases the sisters are far and few between and the brothers outnumber them at least seven to one. So needless to say I prefer the love and strength of African American women. And I'm not saying that there is anything wrong with dating outside of your race. I'm saying that I prefer to share my time, my attention, my effort, and my love for women with someone who has a vested interest in the plight that we share as African Americans.

African American women possess assets that are not common among all women. The African American woman's plight is just as difficult as the African American man's if not more. African American women are usually more so than not, the casualty of our own inability to be the men we need to be. They bear the burden of our failures and flaws more so than we do through raising our children alone, acting as the provider, the protector, the teacher, and the head of the household. Some would say that their predicament is no more of a burden than that of a Caucasian woman or any other woman. The difference is we as men have served as the adversary of our women instead of their allies. Unfortunately because of the emotional state of most women, these types of issues become concerns when trying to establish and maintain a viable relationship when women do meet men like myself. Once again let me clarify my position: by no means am I claiming to be a godsend but what I am saying is that men like myself and others, men who are making an effort to transform the way we think and live our lives for the greater good of us, tend to carry the weight of the emotional, psychological, and physical baggage caused by those less socially, psychologically, politically, and economically conscious than others. *And we call ourselves men!* How can we attempt to call ourselves men if in the same breath we can tell our women that they have nothing to offer us because they bear the responsibility of raising their children alone because another so-called man couldn't or wouldn't live up to what he should be? Women should also understand that just as we have a responsibility in being better men, our women must also make an honest effort in being better women. I know, I know, here it comes! You can't expect men to bear the weight of doing what's right without expecting the same of our counterparts. When it comes to relationships the role our women play is just as vital as the role we must play. This concept is most important as it pertains to women who use failed or poor relationships from the past as a justification for an inability to recognize and establish a functional and meaningful relationship.

Women don't own the patent or copyrights to heartache and pain. I know it's hard for our egos to own up to it but we share some of the same emotions as our women counterparts. We just process and express it differently. As we look at ourselves, men and women, we must evaluate our strengths and weaknesses as they pertain to relationships. If we can minimize our weaknesses and maximize our strengths as they pertain to relationships, then we can take a balanced approach to establishing and maintaining a workable companionship. All this sounds like a lot of hard work and thinking through, and sometimes it is, but really it's not if you've taken the time to get to know yourself as an individual. Who knows you better than you? Who knows what you really like and dislike in a relationship better than you? These very things are the things we fail to think about when we buy that drink at the bar or when we exchange our phone numbers at least two or three times that evening at the club. Women use past relationships to justify their lack of appreciation, trust, and faith in men, when in reality; it should be the exact opposite.

As we experience certain things in our life our expectations should change. For example, if we encounter a relationship where there is a lack of affection, attention, or any other desired emotion or behavior, then the expectation for the next relationship should be what was lacking in the previous relationship. When the same mistakes are made over and over again we tend to get caught up in relationships that have no apparent future and are considered to be a waste of time. Unfortunately it's expected that every man should suffer for the misguided ill-intent of others. In light of my sarcasm this has become all too common in African American relationships. Men who have some sense of decency and integrity (and, yes, there are men out there like that!) are constantly being held accountable for the insecurities of women. If we understand nothing else about women we must understand this; women are emotional by nature and are very insecure. The emotional roller coaster they ride is something we'll never be able to control. But we use their insecurities as weapons rather than tools.

Let's look at this point a little closer. Society as a whole has played on women's insecurities for as long as we can remember. I've always said that if I could think of a way to exploit the insecurities of women on a large scale I would be a very rich man. Think about it, cosmetic surgery, diets, hair weaves, clothes—all exploit the insecurities of women. Women call them enhancements, I call them insecurities. If it looks like a duck and sounds like a duck, then it's probably a duck! That's where women are most vulnerable. We as men use these insecurities as weapons against women to control or harm them rather than tools to make them better. When we tell the mother of our children that another man would never take her seriously because she has children or when we fail to make our women feel like they're valued and respected not only in our eyes but in the eyes of others, then we're using those insecurities to control and harm them. When we consider our roles as men we should understand that it is our responsibility to strengthen our women, not to weaken them, and to guide them, not control them. We can never expect women to feel secure in allowing us to be the men we need to be until we can make them feel secure with themselves first and then with the idea of having a *Better Man.* A lot of times women can't differentiate between a better man and any other man until they've been manipulated, exploited, and taken advantage of. These are the type of situations and conditions in which we strive to be better. And it's understandable that these same insecurities our women endure probably originate from previous relationships and we should exercise patience and be able to empathize with our counterparts; but on the other hand, should we also be held liable for the actions of others? It has become commonplace that better men pay for the mistakes of others. In such events, one man can make a woman despise all men for an extended period of time. In these cases women make critical errors in judgment when they allow their past to get in the way of what is apparent in the present. I've always said, "Show me a strong, independent black woman and I'll show you a bag lady," a woman with so much emotional and psychological baggage that she appears homeless. And in a sense she is—she has no emotional or psychological stability, like a homeless person without a stable place to live. Bag ladies tend to miss out on opportunities because of the baggage they carry. They allow the baggage they carry to become barriers in establishing and sustaining something meaningful and worthwhile. If patience is a virtue then exercising patience with a bag lady is a miracle. Relationships are hard enough to develop without having to cope with the weight of psychological and emotional baggage. These types of relationships are the most difficult to establish because of the lack of trust in the concept of having a better man.

There is one thing that those of us who strive to be better men should be aware of when it comes to relationships; not every woman is going to be receptive to a better man. The concept is virtually foreign to them. I know this sounds amazingly odd but it's true. As was stated before, it's unfortunate that it's usually the better man who suffers for the misguided ill-intent of others. The insecurities and emotions that were discussed earlier are the primary reason for these types of occurrences. Women look for that myth of a man being generally good in nature, so when they consistently find disappointment and discontent with the state of relationships, it presents an uphill battle for those of us who are genuine in nature and are sincere in spirit. They say if something is too good to be true, then it probably is. Well, when a good human being, a good person, a better man is evident in your eyes, then it's the exact opposite, it's probably true! Being single without children and having a professional career, you would think it would be quite easy finding a mate who would be open to developing a relationship. I mean isn't that what women say they want? Come on, an educated, professional, decent-looking single man with no children and making an effort to do what's right and be a better man? That's not too good to be true and I don't think it's too much to ask for. It's what should be expected. I'm sure I speak for a number of men when I say it can be truly frustrating being looked upon as someone who can't relate to having or raising children so it's impossible to understand how or what it takes to raise them. It can also be truly disturbing to be looked upon as an individual who can't be in an established, committed, and monogamous relationship because of a lack thereof. It's that exact type of frustration that inspired me to want to be a better man, a better person, the man I need to be.

I really didn't take relationships seriously until I met what I believed to be my soul mate. We complemented each other in every way possible. For me the perfect definition of soul mates would be two individuals who are immediately drawn to each other through a favorable attraction and who find a mutual understanding or acceptance of each other regardless of his or her faults or weaknesses. Individuals as such tend to find themselves connected in some shape or form for a lifetime. Where I was strong, she was weak and in turn where she was strong I was weak. I don't think you meet those types of individuals often and when you do you know it, understand it, and embrace it. Meeting her played a very big part in motivating me into wanting to be a better man. She also gave me some of the inspiration for this book. Meeting her was a godsend because it made me a better person, a better human being, and a better man. I'm not really sure if every man has a soul mate and if we do I'm really not sure if we're fortunate enough to actually meet them. But it's unfortunate that I had to meet her in order for a metamorphosis of wanting to be better to occur. That's why it's important for us to understand how being the men we are impacts others, including the people we come in contact with. The impact she made on my life was instrumental in my desire to be better. It's so very important that we understand this point because if we look at the state of our society—the African American community—we lack influence and guidance in so many ways. I don't know if she understood what kind of impact she had on my life and the man I've evolved into but if she did I'm sure she'd be proud to know that just giving me the opportunity to know, understand, and appreciate her made me a better person and a better man. A good woman can bring out the best in a man and the same can be said about a good man. In focusing on this side of the spectrum, we should understand the value of the women we choose to associate or deal with. We have to consider the things we have to offer our women that are intangible, and the same has to be considered when we find interest in a potential mate, partner, or what have you. When seeking a possible mate we should consider those who have the potential to bring out the best in us. Meaning, when a man seeks a woman and in turn a woman seeks a man, we should be very mindful of those who have something to offer that makes us not only a better man or woman, but a better person as well. Those who have our best interest at heart tend to bring out the best in us. These types of individuals encourage and build our character, self-esteem, and confidence. These are the individuals who provide constructive influence as opposed to endowing us with destructive persuasion. For those of us who have been fortunate enough to have met and experienced an individual of this caliber, we can attest to the significance of such qualities in a mate. If a potential mate or partner has nothing to offer in terms of the intangible things that make us better as men and women, then these individuals should be considered expendable. Granted, if we all have something to offer in some way, shape, form, or fashion, then we should be vigilant in whom we choose to associate ourselves with. And I don't mean what individuals bring to the table materially; I mean what we all have to bring to the table emotionally, psychologically, and spiritually. If you can't make your mate or partner better in some way, then why make the effort? Settling has no place in being better. And if that is what we strive to be as men, then know and understand when better becomes settling. Even then, when we look at a potential partner or soul mate there are certain things we should consider.

We all make decisions that are contrary to what's best for us, but when looking at a potential companion we have to be honest with ourselves as well as with the individuals we choose to deal with. We all have an idea of the type of individual who is considered appealing to us and what we should all understand is that what we like is not always what's necessarily best for us. So with that being said, we have to come to a realization and make the choice that's not only going to make us happy at the end of the day, but what is also in our own best interest. Now of course there are consequences to the choices we make and we should know that to choose the act is to choose the consequences. Accepting responsibility and accountability for the choices we make is a sign of growth and maturity, whether it's at work, at home, or within a relationship. Once you go outside that box of your ideal mate or partner, you run the risk of opening yourself up to repercussions. A lot of times we make choices that are not in our own best interest but are in the best interest of others. These types of choices often lead to serious ramifications that create barriers to developing meaningful relationships with someone who has our best interest in mind.

As the focus is not totally on the role that women play

in our relationships, an even greater focus should be placed on the shortcomings of men and our role in creating dysfunctional relationships. I often find it amusing when men, especially African American men, expect their women, or even women they deal with in general, to play their role in the relationship. When I say their role, I'm referring to the role of the head of household, protector, provider, and teacher. I sometimes wonder what kind of man would expect his woman or any other woman to pull the load and take on more responsibility than he should. Somehow the idea of such a notion is totally absurd to me. One can only speculate as to what kind of things such an individual has been exposed to. Whatever these things are, they're the type of things that we strive to overcome. As men we should understand that most if not all women want men. If our women have to carry the bulk of the load in our relationships, why do they need us? What's most difficult about this concept is that a lot of times just as we don't realize our roles in relationships, women don't understand their roles in relationships as well. Just as we've lacked guidance and influence, we should imagine that our counterparts have been lacking the same. Understanding that the lack of modeling for women is just as important as our lack thereof is of consequence to us all. We often find that women are conditioned to be independent of viable relationships. It's unfortunate but it's also very understandable to think that just as men are taught to exploit and manipulate others, women are predisposed to the same type of negative behaviors. In striving to be better I think it's safe to presume that a better man would desire a better woman in return. With that being said, it's important that in leading by example we lead the way for our women to follow in being better. When we earn the respect needed for our women to admire, trust, and believe in us, it's considered to be instrumental in allowing them to allow us to lead. We can trust in the view that no woman wants a man who is considered weak. Show me a woman who wants a man who is weak in stature and character, and it's representative of a lack of understanding of not only what a better man is, but what a man in general should be. Using profanity or cursing your woman or any other woman and controlling her through threats, disrespect, and physical intimidation does nothing more than validate your inability to guide and influence her through love, patience, and direction. It's extremely easy to subject others to fear and intimidation rather than influencing them through modeling and teaching. Not only women but people in general can admire someone or something they can learn from. Even so, the insecurities of men play an even greater role in how effective our relationships are, more so than those of women. Just as a man should understand that women are emotional and insecure, women should understand that men have egos along with their insecurities. Unfortunately it's the emotions that make women's insecurities much more complex.

I guess one might ask how can one be more complex than the other. Well, egos create stubbornness and inflexibility. These particular traits make it difficult for a man to place a woman in a position that puts her foremost. Unfortunately because of our past, women have taken on the role of the primary provider, protector, teacher, and head of household. This role makes it very difficult for men to develop into what we need to be. Because of the male ego and our insecurities there are barriers that have to be hurdled more often than not. When women have had to take on these types of roles it makes it very difficult for them to relinquish that role even when there is a potentially better man willing to assume these same duties. Women often feel a loss of control whereas they were in total control of every aspect of their lives beforehand. Being that it is just as difficult for men to embrace the same concept, if you think about it, when women are sustaining and maintaining an entire household and have taken on the aforementioned roles, why would they relinquish that type of control? Mind you, when I use the word control I'm not alluding to the physical sense of the word. I'm referring to the responsibility of guiding, developing, and influencing all that we are responsible for. If we've failed to step up to the plate and be the men we need to be, why should we expect any woman to give up that role? Any man who feels comfortable with being in a relationship where the woman has taken on his role, the role of the provider, protector, teacher, and head of the household, has no sense of who he is or what he should be. This type of mentality is indicative of a man who has been misguided or is uneducated. This is why it's so important to start with us. And just as it is important to start with us, it is just as important to understand that having a false sense of reality is damaging to what we aspire. What comes with a false sense of reality are unrealistic expectations that create disappointment and despair. And what is meant by a false sense of reality is the perception that men that are considered good in nature, are born that way.

Becoming a better man takes effort and hard work. So it is unrealistic to think that a man who is considered better in nature is without fault. Remember that the reality is that we are all men and we make mistakes. Our morals and values are taught and molded from birth. So if what we're taught is to lie, cheat, manipulate, and exploit to achieve our goals, then it'll take just as much effort to learn the opposite. Our morals and values don't necessarily come from teachings alone. A lot of times we allow our morals and values to be shaped by unfavorable experiences or negative encounters with different individuals. So it would be wise to say that people and men in particular change because they want to or see a need for it. So as men we can't allow certain individuals or experiences to dictate who we are. Who we are is what makes us stand out from others. This is most evident in the way we view our relationships with our counterparts. Women should understand that better men weren't always better. The same man you revere had to make mistakes before he was able to learn and understand the role he plays in relationships. It takes a lot of guidance, along with trial and error, to achieve a balanced approach to being the men we need to be, and it's going to take as much patience and understanding from our counterparts in order to achieve the overall target.

One of the most difficult aspects of being a better man in relationships is maintaining a certain degree of integrity. We all know that we can't control the actions of others but we can all be well aware of our own actions and the consequences that may come along with them. So what makes a better man better is his ability to exceed the expectations of the norm. In saying this, one of the primary perceptions that our female counterparts have of men in general and African American men in particular is that we manipulate and exploit women for our own personal gain and secondly, that we're uncontrollably promiscuous and it's impossible for us to remain monogamous. Needless to say, arguing these points would be moot. But what I will say is that in becoming a better man there are certain expectations that can't be eluded. Better men are transparent in nature. What I mean by that is, what you see is what you get. There aren't any obstacles of deception. There is no need for manipulation or exploitation of others for personal gain because the intent of a better man is not for personal gain. Being a better man means considering others before you consider yourself. Remember, your objective is for the common good of us—all of us, not just one's self. It's understandable that this is a difficult task but that's why it's called being a *Better Man* because most men can't or won't accomplish it or even attempt it for that matter. When we're honest and forthcoming it's indicative of being unselfish. It is often difficult for women and men alike to accept the truth as it really is. Being honest and forthcoming allows others to make decisions based on truthfulness and not deception. So if the intent is not consistent with what is considered to be better, then potential female associates, whether they are casual relationships or something more formal, should be given the opportunity to have what's in the best interest of all parties to be taken into consideration and let choices be made based on facts, not what is perceived to be real. Some may disagree with this point of view, but when you're honest, transparent, and forthcoming you negate your responsibility in the outcome of choices that are made by others. There are many who would argue this point and of course most of the participants would be of the opposite sex. But if we are to take responsibility and be held accountable for the choices we make, then so should the recipients of our honesty and transparency. To sum up, regardless of which gender is the facilitator, once an individual has been honest and genuine in expressing their intent, then they should not be held accountable or responsible for the choices of others because they've allowed others to make their choices based on honesty and truthfulness. In the end, we are accountable and responsible for our own decisions when it comes to our relationships! We shouldn't blame others for the outcomes of the decisions we make.

When we ponder the thought of entering into a relationship there are certain aspects that should be addressed before investing our time, effort, attention, and emotions. One should consider the state of consciousness of one's intended person of interest. Just because we strive to be better men, that doesn't necessarily mean that our better halves are equally as mindful. In theological terminology it's referred to as being equally yoked. Which simply suggests that you should pursue someone with equal interest as yourself and equally conscious of the same ideas and ideals. As we scrutinize our relationships as they are today we oftentimes find some of our female counterparts to be less aware than we are in attempting to be better men. You'd think that just striving to be better would be enough. Unfortunately there are certain cases in which just being better is just not enough. There are certain instances where material gratification may be the primary factor in basing a relationship upon for some of our better halves who may be less conscious than ourselves. In theses instances we find that our women counterparts value our material status above our ability to exhibit a genuine, sincere care and concern for them. Understanding that these instances can be frustrating and downright offensive at times, there have to be boundaries set on our part. These types of interests can be found in a variety of women regardless of their demographic makeup. Being aware that there is not an abundance of us with unlimited resources, somehow we've lost sight of what is really relevant. We've let status symbols and material things become the gauge by which our sincerity and our ability to be genuine are measured. Sometimes as better men we get caught up in the allure of utilizing flashy, material, and big-ticket items to attract the attention of those we desire. A lot of times we aspire to attract the attention of the opposite sex with hopes of appealing to them physically or intimately. These types of relationships usually result in a temporary infatuation that ends in another squandered investment. For the most part, better men usually lack the resources to attract certain types of women anyway. It's rare that you find a man of this caliber combined with the resources to match. I'm not saying that these instances don't occur, but they are considered to be a rarity. We lack certain resources because it is not the primary objective of better men to gain fame and fortune.

In reiterating the purpose, the intent is to be a better man, not only for ourselves but for our women, children, and family as a whole. So let's not misconstrue "better" to mean more money or fame and fortune. Granted, there is nothing wrong with having an overabundance of resources to provide for your family. But having unlimited resources is not the norm for better men and does not necessarily make you a better man. It just makes you a man with unlimited resources. There are several better men who can be considered an exception to the rule but they're definitely not the majority or the norm. Be that as it may, when our female counterparts seek to attain resources over substance, then that issue becomes theirs, not ours. There is one thing that we definitely can't allow and that's permitting others to make their issues our issues. I'm not speaking of issues we help create through our inability to be better men. The opportunity for fame and fortune is not afforded to everyone. If that were the case, there would be no need for economic development in the lives of the less fortunate. So we should be aware of falling into the pitfall of making someone else's shallow and superficial desires ours. It's truthful to say that finances are an important part of a relationship just as it is equally important in the everyday lives of all of us, but it shouldn't be the sole foundation on which a relationship is based.

I understand that we are all human and as humans we are all subject to faults and weaknesses. And as we strive to be better men we're not exempt from fault, weaknesses, or failure for that matter. But having faults and weaknesses and being subject to failure does not have to compromise our objective in becoming better men in our relationships and how we treat our women. It's difficult to take the high road sometimes, especially when you're involved with a mate or a partner who is less conscious than you are. This becomes extremely complicated when confronted with making the determination between what is considered to be the best decision versus what is considered to be the right decision. It's challenging for most men and for most people in general for that matter to determine the distinction between the best decision and the right decision when it comes down to relationships, not only with our women but with relationships in general. This is most evident when we are confronted with doing what's right versus doing what's best. It would seem that as we strive to be better men, this quandary would hardly be considered an issue. It would be rational to think that obviously as better men, when we strive to do what is right day in and day out, making the decision that is considered to be right would be our primary instinct. Life would be a lot less difficult if it was just that easy. But if you've lived the life that we've lived as men, then you know that life is just not that simple. And for us as African American men it's even more difficult because of the circumstances in which we live and how we develop our relationships. It's hard for better men to accept that the right decision may not always be the best decision, especially when it comes to relationships. Making the right decision rarely encompasses what is best. I would argue that this is because what's best can be viewed as being very subjective. When subjectivity is involved, what's best may be skewed by emotions and biased perceptions. Whereas what is considered right is usually concrete and is supported by a common belief system such as laws, guide-lines, or values. For some it's often difficult to differentiate between the two but for others it can be effortless.

One example we all may be able to relate to is the deci-sion to commit to the mother of our children regardless of our lack of genuine, sincere care and concern for her. This example poses the query of whether or not this is the right decision or is this decision best. As we said before, the right decision may not always be the best decision. Mor-ally, the right decision would be to commit to the mother of your child or children in order to establish a foundation that is conducive to the growth and development of a functional family, made up of a mother and a father, with the father figure as the teacher, protector, provider, and head of household. The best decision may be for the male figure to not commit himself to something that he lacks the inner spirit to obligate himself to.

Another example that we may all be able to relate to is the quandary of disclosing infidelity in a relationship dur-ing a moment of a brief and regrettable indiscretion. Should what's right be considered when what's right could ulti-mately end your relationship, which you both value, or is it best that the one brief indiscretion be withheld for the wel-fare of the relationship? I know some would argue that what's right is black and white; there is no subjectivity in-volved. But what about what's best? Remember, we are all human! And if what's right is what's right, then there's a black book that says we should forgive and love, as he forgives and loves us. As you can see, these are just some of the issues that we are faced with as we strive to become better men. And as better men we're obligated to consider these things as we transcend the normal expectations of what is currently considered to be a man.

There are certain things we should never consider doing as we attempt to be better men. One thing we should never generally do as men and even more so as better men in particular is enter into any kind of relationship under false pretenses. A lot of times this can be attributed to our own selfishness. And as better men we've discussed in general the need for better men to be unselfish. Entering into relationships under false pretenses is usually an indication of deceit, manipulation, and exploitation. When these types of relationships are created, the outcome is typically not favorable for either party. Just as we should not enter into relationships under false pretenses, one of the biggest mistakes we can make as men is taking our significant other for granted. This is seen in various types of relationships from the women we date to the mother of our children and even our wives. As men our egos tend to play a significant role in our inability to appreciate even the smallest aspects of our relationships. The things we take for granted can be considered minute to us as men but can mean the world to the individual with whom we're involved. Ignoring or not paying attention to the little things can cost us an enormous loss in the end. As better men we're obligated to pay attention to the little things. The little things may consist of the things that mean so much but get so little consideration. Women consider these things to be abstract, meaning things that are not obvious to the eye. These things require effort in order to be recognized. They're usually not visible to the naked eye. But better men seek to discover and identify these things that mean so much to those who should mean even more to us. These are just some of the things that make us better than the men we are. These are the things that women appreciate and find special. No one wants or likes to feel taken for granted, including us as men. But as better men we tend to be taken for granted more so than those who are not as mindful. Being taken for granted tends to not have as much of an impact on us as men because it's typically not in our nature to carry or hold on to emotional or psychological baggage, unlike our female counterparts. Nevertheless, it's understandable to experience similar emotions as do our counterparts. Remember, we do share some of the same emotions; we just tend to express them differently. So, just as we feel unappreciated for our efforts at becoming better men, we should understand that we must be better in modeling the appreciation we seek.

When I said, "With love comes consequences," I couldn't have said it more eloquently. There is a misconception that as men we don't love as often as do women. On the contrary, nothing could be further from the truth. Men do love as frequently as women and when we do, we love remorselessly. And this is not to say that women don't, but it's unfortunate that the consequences of that love have lifelong implications on what type of men we become. As we strive to develop into what is considered to be a better man, there are circumstances that can be considered discouraging. What is important is that we don't allow these discouraging circumstances to dictate who we become as men. A lot of times we allow these circumstances to influence our character or who we are. As better men we shouldn't allow anyone or anything to influence our character. We are who we are, so if you're a better man, a man who is not abusive in nature for example, you shouldn't allow anything or anyone to cause you to act outside of your character. When this is the case you tend to lose sight of who you are and eventually it causes you to lose control over that aspect of your relationship. We'll discuss what happens to men when they feel like they've lost control later. But what does happen is that we make attempts to regain that control without even attempting to understand why we lost the control in the first place. So in order to avoid these types of pitfalls, when we recognize a relationship, situation, or individual that causes us to act outside of our character, meaning the person we really are, then it's time to sever the relationship because our best interest is not being considered. Some say you don't pick who you love. I would beg to differ. I say love is choice. You choose who you decide to love and who not to love. The problem is that we often choose to love those who fail to love us in return. We would all like to be loved the way we love. And when that doesn't occur, the consequences of our choices come into play. The biggest hindrance with being a better man is the perception that a good man is synonymous with a weak man. It's unfortunate that in a society where there is so much manipulation, exploitation, deception, greed, envy, jealousy, and dishonesty, being sincere and genuine, and having a care and concern is considered a weakness. What is even more unfortunate is that when better men open themselves up to dealings or women who are not necessarily ideal in pursing a viable relationship they become vulnerable to deception, manipulation, and exploitation. A prime example is when we as men tend to go outside of our box. We all have an imaginary box that we use to place certain desirable characteristics in when we're looking for a potential mate. This box is more relevant as it pertains to establishing formal relationships versus informal or casual relationships. We use this box to create the ideal mate or what we consider to be the ideal mate. Some men may prefer intelligence, beauty, or a sense of humor while others may prefer an outgoing personality, assertiveness, and ambition. We all have an idea of what type of woman we could consider to be marriage material or at least girlfriend or even relationship potential. Nevertheless, when we go outside of our box we tend to suffer the consequences of it—disappointment. When there are certain environmental factors involved we are predisposed to encountering certain types of individuals. This can be seen in the type of individuals we find ourselves attracted to based on our own circumstances. A lot of times this is more prevalent with our female counterparts but is not uncommon to men. In other words, we tend to settle for less than what we expect. Like I said, this is more common with our female counterparts but it is not uncommon for men, especially better men. A lot of times this is a direct result of the frustrations that come along with establishing the idea of a box that encompasses the perfect mate in the first place. Nevertheless, we all do it at some point or another.

It's important to note that we can't change or make anyone into something or someone they're not. Consider this; we admire certain things about certain women. We look for particular qualities in women when we're considering the aspects of a relationship. These qualities are indicative of our expectations and desires of our ideal mates. Does this mean that every woman we enter into a relationship with is what we wish for or need? Of course not! We as human beings, not just as men, find it hard to accept people for who they are. We tend to think we can change people for the better, whether it's for their benefit or ours. Remember, people change because they see a need for it or because they want to. Even I'm not too presumptuous to think that I can change each and every individual I set out to reach. But what I do know is that I can change me, and if we as men understand that, then we've taken another step in evolving into a better man. It is redundant to say that relationships are hard work but it is profound to state that without them our very existence is less relevant. Let's face it, as much as we'd like to believe that our existence encompasses the center of the universe, the simple fact is that without our female counterparts and the relationships we create with them, whether they are casual or formal, we're not complete in our existence as men without them. Being interdependent upon each other is what makes our relationships durable. Overall it is expected that we provide the example for others to follow and that we lead the way in establishing a foundation for our relationships to nurture. Whether or not we accept this responsibility is a choice but the expectation remains the same. It is inevitable that if relationships aren't worked at and are not nurtured then they will come to an unfortunate demise. This can be seen in all types of relationships, whether they are formal or casual.

The one thing that we all know is constant is change. Change is a way of life and should be embraced and not rejected. So when our relationships change and we try to resist the idea, we should consider it as the process of growth and grasp it. We can never forget how much work relationships are and how important it is that we understand that so that we have realistic expectations. When dealing with human beings, especially those who are as diverse as we are, we shouldn't expect our relationships to be as unproblematic as others. Our relationships with our women are predisposed to issues and concerns that have plagued our community psychologically, socially, politically, and economically from past and present generations. Things that are simplistic for others may not be as simple for us. Because our plight differs from others, our coping skills are dissimilar. Within our relationships we may address social, political, psychological, and economical issues distinctively. If you take the time, think about how we address money issues with our mates compared to how others address them. Economically we look at our finances with our women as bartering tools. It's always assumed that potential mates are out to manipulate or exploit their positions as women to gain an unfair advantage when it comes to financial gain or even just financial stability. Now take a look at other relationships within other cultures. There appears to be a trust factor that is elusive in the type of relationships we indulge in. Previously we spoke of the psychological issues that we encounter in our relationships. Socially, there is no other culture in our country that has made their women the subject of more ridicule, degradation, and disrespect than ours. It has become more and more evident through the music we listen to and the images we display to not only our women and children but to others as well. Politically, the effects of disenfranchisement have played a critical role in how we interact with our partners in that it causes a separation of ideas and ideals when it comes to how we view our relationships as they pertain to the concepts of everything from marriage, careers, and raising children to establishing the roles in our relationships. It should be our hope and desire to understand these issues and concerns so that we may establish better relationships and so that in turn we may create a better us. These are not just things that others would want from us, but things that we should want for ourselves. The establishment of a viable relationship should be the methodology to create and start a functional family. I know it's become the norm to start a family first and then attempt to establish the relationship but obviously this method has not been very successful for most and almost nonexistent for others. Before we can become better fathers, we must become better men and in turn, establish better relationships. Our methodology has to focus on us as men first, our relationships second, and our children last but not least. For without the first two, our children are destined to continue to be left without our guidance, influence, leadership, understanding, teaching, love, care, and concern. So before we enter into our next relationship let's consider the consequences of our choices and not only that, let's consider the ripple effect that those choices may have on others.

Chapter 3
Like My Daddy

The title of this chapter was not meant to be misleading and by no means is this chapter a dedication to my father. As we reflect on how we were raised as children we often look at the things we enjoyed about our childhood and the things that weren't so enjoyable. A lot of times we tend to hold on to a lot of the negative images of our childhood that cause resentment when it comes to certain situations or issues. Whatever emotional or psychological baggage we carry from our childhood becomes irrelevant when it's our turn to become the provider, the head of the household, teacher, and protector. In the end, what legacy will you leave when your children say the words *Like my daddy*? Every good man wants to hear the words *Like my daddy* come from his child or children. In some ways *Like my daddy* is a sign of approval or validation. When a son or daughter says *Like my daddy* it's an affirmation of the guidance and influence a man has provided for his child. When a little girl says I want a man just *like my daddy* it's indicative of the type of relationship that has been developed between a man and his daughter. The same can be said when a little boy says I want to be just *like my daddy.* Those three little words take on different meanings, depending on the type of man it refers to. Before I elaborate on this point let me clarify something; it is not my intent to degrade, disrespect, or belittle any man of any race, culture, or ethnicity but when an image of crime, abuse, lack of respect, ignorance, and illegal drug usage is portrayed to a child and he wants to emulate that image, then *Like my daddy* takes on a totally different meaning. And it would be the same as if a young girl perceived that image as what she thought a better man should be, *Like my daddy.* When discussing the role we play in the guidance and influence of our children there are several factors that should be considered. If we understand nothing else we should understand this: once children reach adulthood they are responsible and held accountable for the decisions they make. But as the provider, protector, teacher, and head of household, we are responsible for the growth and development that guide and influence their decision-making.

I guess one might think how could someone who hasn't experienced raising children give any guidance on how to be a better father to a child? Well, you don't have to be a parent in order to understand that children are developed, shaped, and molded by the environment in which they are raised. It doesn't take a rocket scientist to figure that one out, but it does take someone with insight into how our values, morals, and knowledge shape the growth and development of our children. Most people, especially men, should want their families, particularly their children, to have a better quality of life than the one they were afforded as a child. In a lot of cases we tend to think that material items constitute a better quality of life. Although some would argue this point, it is conceivable to think that a better quality of life involves much more than just material items. What many people fail to realize is that sometimes things that are tangible are not as relevant as things that are not. This can be seen in the values we instill in our children. For example, in some instances we tend to view giving our children things such as expensive clothing, high-priced toys, and big-ticket items as providing them with a better quality of life when in all actuality, all we're doing is shaping their values to prioritize things that are material and temporary over things that are eternal. Things that are eternal can never be taken away, discarded, or broken. The love for a child is considered to be eternal and can never be taken away, discarded, or broken. The same can be said for education, whether it be formal or informal. So when we think about the future of our responsibilities we should consider things that are eternal versus things that are not. Expressing love, care, and concern for your children is much more than ensuring that they have all the material things they think they need or want. I appreciated the intangible things my mother gave me so much more in the end because it helped make me the man I am today. It wasn't the clothes, the games, and the big-ticket items. I do and did appreciate those things but they didn't and will never compare to the love, caring, and understanding that so many children lack as we stand today. Before we can attempt to be better men to our children we have to acknowledge our responsibility in the roles we play in their lives. I understand that there's a portion of men who may not be touched or encouraged by this insight. But for those who are and for those straddling the fence on being a better man to their children, think about the kind of man your father was to you, if you even knew or know your father. The thought alone is provoking enough to stimulate a conversation in itself. Just as we discussed with other relationships, we usually carry emotional and psychological baggage from our childhood that impacts the way we interact with our own children, if we interact with them at all.

In today's society there are many factors that place children at risk, and growing up without a father is one of the most significant factors. The majority of African American prison inmates were raised fatherless, the majority of African American high school dropouts were raised fatherless, the majority of African American substance abusers were raised fatherless, and the majority of African American households are fatherless. It's obvious that the common denominator is us! Of all the risk factors that impact African American children, this is arguably one of the most relevant. I'm sure many would agree that a child is much more likely to have a more realistic perception of what life should consist of when there is the presence of a man in their lives. Some may even go so far as to say that a Daddy is the first man a little girl falls in love with and the first man a boy learns to respect and emulate. Notice, I used the word "Daddy," not rapper, not athlete, and definitely not the local thug or drug dealer. By all means, there is no disrespect intended to anyone who chooses to be an entertainer, athlete, or career criminal. But the primary responsibility of guiding, influencing, and developing our children lies with us. By not taking an active role in the development, guidance, and influence of our children's lives, we've allowed others to be that role model they so desperately seek when in need. As men our wants and needs drive our motivation and objectives but as fathers our obligations supersede any and everything else. I'm not saying that once you conceive a child your life is over, but your life takes on a totally different meaning, not just for you but for the life you are obligated to. I use the word obligated because it has a very strong connotation. Obligation is synonymous with words such as duty, responsibility, requirement, and commitment.

Once a child is conceived, as a man you are obligated to provide a genuine, sincere care and concern for it. Many men may not believe this to be true but if you have an understanding of what becoming a better man is really about then you will agree. One of the more pressing issues is that we as men tend not to understand the obligations we incur when we have casual sex, unprotected sex, group, or any other kind of sex! Even though the intent is not to conceive a child and the purpose is for pleasure or gratification, every man and even young boy should know that when you have sex there are risks involved that include conceiving a child. And once that child is conceived you are obligated to it. There are economic and psychological ramifications attached to conceiving a child that are not considered when entering into any relationship, whether it's casual or formal. Understanding the role we play as providers, teachers, protectors, and the head of the household is critical to becoming a better man and in turn, a better father. The image we provide for our sons or daughters is what will influence the way they perceive the world to be. If your son sees you as a responsible father providing for himself and his mother while treating her with genuine care and concern, then you've modeled what a man should be to a woman and a child. If you value and emphasize hard work and education, then your son or daughter will value the same concept. The same could be said for the man who shows his child that men should treat women with disrespect, degradation, and abuse. If we provide these images to our children, this is how they will perceive the world to be. It can be said that your children share in your success or failure, so as you strive and achieve they share in your success just as they share in your struggles and shortcomings when you falter or fail. There's no book on this earth that can tell you how to successfully raise a child, because all children are different and each circumstance is unique. But there are fundamental principles that can guide the development and growth of children that will instill basic morals and values that influence their decision-making. Without these fundamental principles children tend to develop morals and values based on external factors that dilute the fabric of their foundation.

So as we look to be better fathers to our children we must first evaluate ourselves and take an inventory of our own self-worth. Regardless of anyone else's perception, we all have something to offer and some value in some shape or form. It's up to us to figure out what we have to offer and maximize it to the fullest. Understanding our weaknesses is just as important as indulging in our self-worth. For understanding our weaknesses is a part of the process of evolving into a better man. For some, our weaknesses are external factors that interfere with the way we perceive ourselves and our environment. For others, our weaknesses are internal and have to be addressed within ourselves. For those of us who have internal as well as external weaknesses acting as barriers to our evolution, the predicament is much more complex. When looking at internal and external weaknesses as they pertain to being a better father we must first evaluate what's within our control. Some may argue that some factors are able to be controlled more so than others. For example, some may say internal factors may be more controllable than external factors because some circumstances that may arise externally may be beyond the scope of our control. We all know that things such as accidents and deliberate interference are beyond our control. But external factors such as the environment in which we live, the women we choose to deal with, the careers and jobs we hold, and the individuals we choose to associate with are all controllable external factors. One very important factor is the part we play as it pertains to children within our lives who are not necessarily ours. We all know and should understand that the role we play in the lives of children who are not necessarily of us is just as essential to us. For those of us who are still single and aspiring to be that better man and eventually a better father, it's unrealistic to think we may never be faced with a situation that may require us to take on the role of provider, teacher, protector, and head of household to the child of another man. These types of relationships are more common than not and should not deter us from achieving our intended goal, which should remain the same regardless of the circumstances. There is no doubt that a relationship that comes with children comes with a greater responsibility. Unfortunately these types of relationships become less attractive because of the implications involved. Anyone who would agree with this perspective should be considered insightful. One could also argue that these types of situations are what make a good man an even better man. It takes a better man to truly accept, love, and care for another man's child as he would his own. This type of relationship is not ordinary. A lot of times these types of relationships lack sincerity and are not genuine. Regrettably, the lack of sincerity and false impressions tend to surface when another child is conceived and there is a disparity in which the siblings are cared for. All too often we see how children not conceived by us are treated, without generosity, sincerity, care, and concern. As we've previously addressed the circumstances of presumably having to raise another man's child, I would be remiss in taking responsibility for us if I didn't reiterate that being that it is already difficult to raise another man's child, it is extremely difficult to not differentiate between your own child and that of another man when involved in relationships. Even so, what's even more important than the role we play in the lives of our child or children is the role we play in the lives of their siblings, particularly when they are not a product of your own creation. The manner in which you treat your child's sibling has a significant effect on how your child views you as a man. I'm not saying that you are obligated to your child's sibling just as you are obligated to your own child—but you do have a responsibility to create a relationship with your child's sibling, whether it's a simple, casual relationship where their presence is acknowledged as a sibling or just modeling what a better man is and should be for them. It's obvious what type of impact it plays on any woman who desires to have a better man for herself and for her children. Regardless of whether or not your child's sibling is your child, you have to realize and understand the relationship your child has with his or her sibling. If you know and understand how your child feels about his or her sibling, then you are obligated to make his or her sibling feel comfortable with your relationship and with your presence in both of their lives.

Anyone who has grown up in a household where there are different fathers can easily relate to this point but for those who were raised by one father in one household it may be difficult to view these circumstances with some form of empathy. If the relationship between your child and his or her sibling is important to them, then it should be even more important to you because you should have a vested interest in the same relationship because of your child. It's extremely difficult for women to trust us with their lives and it's even more difficult for them to trust us with the lives of their children. So the term *Like My Daddy* becomes more than just a validation of the relationship and the guidance you've provided for a child, it becomes the very pinnacle of the influence you've established with that child. *Like My Daddy* means so much more when it comes from another man's child. Many would be hard-pressed to disagree with this point of view and I'm not sure why anyone would want to. It's certainly understandable to have reservations about entering into a relationship that comes along with the responsibility of raising another man's child but there should also be some kind of consideration in what kind of impact you may play in the lives of those you touch.

Oftentimes as I grew up I wondered what it was like to be *Like My Daddy.* When we choose not to be the fathers we need to be, there are insurmountable repercussions. Before we get bewildered with excuses let's clarify one thing: not being a father to your child is a choice, nothing more, nothing less. Most men tend to shy away from responsibilities they feel they had no part in creating. And just as it takes a special kind of man to take on a venture of this magnitude, it takes a man just as special to choose not to. So understand this if nothing else, for those of us who choose not to be a father to our children the damage and harm you create is intangible and ultimately detrimental to the growth and development of the children we raise. It's realistic to assume that if a man chooses not to be a father to his child, then any kind of damage or harm that may come of it is irrelevant to him. But for those of us who do choose to be fathers, there is a gratification that transcends anything within our reach. And for those of us who choose to be a father to another man's child, the reward is even greater. Making another man's child your own is a feat that is unparalleled. Children are very perceptive, especially children who have been deprived of sincerity, generosity, care, and concern. It becomes imperative when establishing a relationship that we not only place our women foremost, but if children are involved, then they should be prioritized as well. Raising children of your own is difficult enough so, needless to say, raising children who are not your own is much more difficult.

Just as there are expectations of male and female relationships, there are expectations of relationships between children and their father. For me, my expectations were very minimal because I had nothing in comparison. My expectations came from different men who came in and out of my life. It was disappointing because none of them had a relationship with my mother. When I say that, I mean I met my role models through life experiences. I took what was good in certain men and I digested it. The things I considered bad, I left behind. I had to know or be taught what was actually good and what was actually bad. That's why I contend that children are very perceptive and we as men should be aware of that realization. In some ways children who have been manipulated and exploited for whatever reason have more insight than adults do. So when we enter into relationships that involve children we should consider the plight of the child or children as well as that of the woman we choose. The effort we put into establishing a relationship with the women who are the subject of our interest should be equally placed on the child or children who comes along with them.

I may not have raised a child, but I was a child once and I've seen men who were insincere, not genuine, manipulative, and exploitive. So not having children does not necessarily make me an amateur; all it does is make me unfortunate. And for those who beg to differ, I say blessings are taken for granted every day. If you have children, appreciate them for what they are, a blessing that is eternal and never temporary. As we go through life and we prioritize what's most important to us, we have a tendency of letting things that are physically gratifying take precedence over things that are indefinable—the things we impart to our children, like communication, time, affection, discipline, and structure. When it comes to our children and the relationships we develop with them, it's so important to recognize that it takes more than just financial support to raise a child. A lot of times we see financial support as being the primary necessity in the upbringing of a child. But the indefinable things are much more relevant when it comes to guiding, shaping, and developing children. The financial support provided by government assistance or an absent father fails in comparison when it comes to what is necessary and in the best interest of our children. Some say the best thing you could do for a child is love its mother. Well, I guess in the same sense, the same could be said about loving a child's father.

Even with this being said there is something we should all consider as men and especially as fathers to our children. For my entire life I've met and talked with individuals who know or have known my father. There has not been, at any place or any time, anything of substance to say about the man who helped conceive me. As I think about it, all my life I've always heard "I know your father," and "You look exactly like your father!" I've never heard, "Your father was a good man" or "Your father did this or your father did that." I'm not saying that my father never achieved or accomplished anything in his lifetime but if he did I'm not aware of it and it appears that not many other people are either, at least none that I've met. I'm not expressing this to take a cheap shot at my father. My point is this: what will be the legacy you leave behind for your child? What will be said about you as a man, a husband, or a father? This is a question we should all consider as we take responsibility for us. This is a question we should pose to those who are less aware or conscious of what our objectives should be, and to those we choose to attempt to guide and influence. If nothing else we should make an effort to be better than what was presented to us as role models, providers, protectors, and heads of households. These are the things we must be in order for us to evolve into the men our children not only want, but need us to be. Think about this, we can all agree that we all want or should want our children to have a better quality of life than the life we live or lived. This is arguably undisputable and as well it should be. But let's make sure we consider the development, guidance, and influence we provide that comes along with that better quality of life. It's understandable that every man can't possess the patience of a Martin Luther King or the dedication of an El-Hajj Malik El-Shabazz. It's not necessary for you to be famous and recognizable among a nation of millions in order to be a better man. What is important is that we leave behind a legacy for our children that acknowledges us as being better men not only in their eyes, but in the eyes of others as well.

There are several fallacies about African American men

and fatherhood that have baffled me as I observe relationships between men and their children and African American men in particular. But there are several concepts that are not fallacies and are just plain ole absurd. One of the most puzzling thus far is the refusal to provide influence, guidance, financial, and emotional support to our child or children out of rejection from a failed relationship. Whether the relationship was causal or something more concrete, the whole idea is completely and utterly unexplainable. I've tried time and time again to understand this concept and I've yet to grasp it. Are we to understand that if the mother of our child or children chooses not to continue to pursue a relationship with us as men, we're entitled to dissolve any type of relationship with our child or children, be it financial or emotional, due to the lack of interest by a mate or partner? Not only is this destructive, it's unbelievable! How can we possibly take such a position when it comes to not only taking responsibility for ourselves but for what and who we are obligated to. *And We Call Ourselves Men!* In instances such as this we must be careful of the bridges we burn. More times than not we make decisions or choices that become harmful in maintaining viable relationships not only with the mother of our children but with our children themselves. In most instances once that bridge is burned, it can be one of the most difficult aspects of a bond to repair when trying to establish a foundation from which to work when developing a relationship with a child. This can be seen from both sides of the spectrum. The same can be said when children burn bridges with their parents and fathers in particular. The relationships between fathers and their children are already tenuous. And creating barriers to the development or improvement of these same relationships does nothing more than hinder the process of developing a healthy rapport. The type of man who negates his responsibility for his child or children based on the rejection of a woman is totally opposite of what we strive to be as better men. On the contrary, the better man accepts what he is responsible for and embraces it. These are the types of issues that test the very constitution of our manhood. This point is not exclusively directed towards just African American men but for all men in general. This type of man is far less exceptional than the average simply because his presence in the life of his child is strictly based upon specific conditions. Our presence, influence, and guidance in the life of our child or children must be unconditional. These types of situations play a part in the way our children perceive not only us as fathers but how they perceive themselves as well. These factors contribute to the development or lack thereof in the way our children view manhood, fatherhood, and family as a whole. Considering this, we shouldn't wonder how so many of our children fall short of the basic skills necessary just to cope with the day-to-day stressors of life. It's the absence of what we should consider to be the backbone of their very existence. This condition becomes most relevant as our children progress through the adolescent stages of development. Albeit just as significant during the early stages of development, the adolescent stage is when children tend to be influenced through external ideals and peer pressure. Often we open our eyes and wonder what happened to the child we thought we raised to be respectful, kind, and courteous. The role we play as the protector, provider, teacher, and head of household becomes even more important as the children we raise develop into the young adults we create. So the absence of our presence as men because of the rejection of a failed relationship is once again something we have to take responsibility for and inevitably be held accountable for. This is something most men rarely even consider, so being conscious of it is unthinkable. Better men are usually conscious of the consequences of a failed relationship as it pertains to the child or children involved. It's those of us who are less cognizant of the ramifications of our actions that impede upon our evolution as being better. The thought alone can breed pessimism for the growth and development of what is considered to be our future.

As we look at the state of our children in the world in which we currently live, we have to ponder the question "What happened?" I would argue that the absence of us as better men can be attributed to the demise of the moral fiber that is lacking in the future of the generations of us. Being in the position that I'm fortunate enough to be in, I've had the opportunity over the last eight to ten years to work with hundreds of children of all ages and of both genders. What's been the most consistent risk factor that has contributed to the impairment of our growth as better men to our children is the absence of us as father figures. Like I said before in Chapter 1, growing up without a father or a father figure isn't anything new to African Americans. Unfortunately as we've seen the world evolve into the state it is currently in, we've failed to adapt to the current set of risk factors that impact the way our children are being raised. The resiliency we've been known to personify has been depleted in the face of adversity. The same risk factors that were faced 20 years ago have multiplied while our desire to overcome them has become stagnant. This is evident by the increase in the disproportionate amount of African American men imprisoned, unemployed, uneducated, and drug addicted. I can't begin to explain how, but somehow, somewhere, we became complacent and uninspired. Our work ethic is little too nonexistent. We don't value things like fatherhood, relationships, manhood, integrity, education, family, and community. These are the things that are not being modeled for our children. Not just our own children, but others as well. Seeing Daddy get up and go to work every day and watching him come back home at night is far from what our children witness. What statistics won't show or tell us are the mothers that we've had the misfortune of witnessing work 50 to 60 hours a week preparing to ensure that our children have what they need, not necessarily what they want, but exactly what they need just to go to school and attempt to focus on learning what other children are taking advantage of. Another thing statistics won't show or tell us is the number of mothers who work overtime ten to 20 hours a week during the holidays so that our children not only have what they need but what they want as well. Notice in both of these instances I mentioned the word *mothers*. At no point did I reference the word *father* or *daddy*. Understanding these instances makes me ask the question "Where are we?" Where are the better men? In most if not all of these occurrences we're nowhere to be found. The ripple effect we've created seems irreversible, not only for our children but for our families as well. Please don't misunderstand this point to be pessimistic. The point was made to be alarming not cynical. Sometimes it takes someone or something to ring the alarm in order for us to awake and open our eyes. For some it may take a simple word or two and for others it may take the degradation and humiliation of an entire generation to ring the alarm. These ideas are a testament of examples we set for our children as men, not necessarily as better men, but as men in general. So when we discuss the development, guidance, and influence we bestow upon our children, let's converse about our duty in taking responsibility for them as well as for us.

I often find it amusing when discussing the development, guidance, and influence we provide for our children. What I've found is that in a lot of cases, when we're not aware of or fully informed of how the world works, we tend to make decisions that are not in the best interest of our children. I would like to think that as men we would all like to see our children enjoy that better quality of life than we did. But what that means is that we have to put ourselves in a better position in order to provide them with that quality of life. What is just as important is the manner in which we raise our children. Sometimes we have the tendency of being a bit overprotective of our children in an attempt to shield them from harm. There are also times when we encourage rapid development and independence, which creates adverse effects as it pertains to the actual maturity of the child. In both cases there are developmental consequences that can cause irreversible damage as we attempt to overcompensate for what we feel was lacking in our own childhood relationships. The objective is to find a balanced approach in achieving pro-social development.

A lot of times we see parents neglect the basic necessities of childhood development either for a lack of knowledge or inadequate resources and sometimes both. As better men it is our responsibility to take the lead in the development of our children. What that means is that sometimes we have to be the bad guy and make some difficult decisions. Making everything that's wrong seem right includes making the tough choices when it comes to the guidance and influence of our children. We all know that there is no surefire way to successfully raise children but there are some things we can do in order to reduce the risk of certain factors. In taking responsibility for us and our children there is one thing that should be understood: schools and the government are not primarily responsible for the guidance, influence, and development of our children. When we send our children to school we send them with the expectation that they will be provided with a formal education facilitated by a professional teacher who has also been formally educated in the development and the teaching of others. Although character development may be incorporated in the educational curriculum, it is not necessarily a requirement. Character development is the responsibility of parents and as men it is more so ours as opposed to others. Teachers and administrators are not obligated to teach our children the basic pro-social skills that are necessary to effectively function in society as a whole. It is our obligation as fathers and better men to take responsibility for us and our children. Attributes such as respect for authority and others, good manners, discipline, and structure are all traits that are all considered necessary in order to just be able to function from day to day in our society as a whole. These are just some of the things that should be taught, modeled, and reinforced as fathers for our children to emulate. Yet we send our children to school lacking these basic skills and expect the teachers to be able to provide them with a foundation for learning. The foundation should be formed by the provider, the teacher, protector, and head of household.

The same could be said for our justice system. It is not the responsibility of the government or justice system to guide, teach, and model what we've failed to do as better men and fathers in general. We've made it acceptable for our children to be taken away and out of our households and raised by the government or the justice system in a manner contrary to what is considered the best interest of our children. And what's in the best interest of our children is to admire us as fathers and better men in providing them with guidance, influence, love, and respect along with the foundation of a functional family setting. When we fail to take responsibility for us and our children we subject them to society's prejudiced perceptions of what society as a whole perceives us to be. Every time we fail to take the time to attend open house meetings at our children's school, call their teachers to inquire about their progress, or fall short of not defending our children on their behalf, we allow injustices to occur that may be disadvantageous to the development and progress of our children at becoming social and productive adults. Certainly, as fathers and as better men if we don't become the protector and voice for our children at a time when they can't speak for themselves, we jeopardize our ability to be those better men and in turn those better fathers that we need to be to our children. In our absence we've allowed others to unfairly persecute and demean our children while leaving our children without recourse. And this is exactly what has taken place, "our absence." We've been pretty much nonexistent for much too long. The responsibility has fallen on the mothers of our children and it has become the norm. This can be seen from the classroom to the courtroom, and if we allow others to take on our role and dictate who or what our children are or become, we've not only failed them but we've failed us as a whole.

One thing we can do as men is emphasize the value of education and learning. As was stated previously, we all know that a lack of education is a handicap that makes it difficult to be successful when competing with others. So as men first and as fathers second, let's start with the education of our children so that they may have the basic skills in order to be functional as people in general. This has to be stressed from day one. As a child, everything should be a learning experience. I'm not referring to teaching our children profanity or the latest rap song. I understand that profanity is almost a common way of communicating in a lot of households. But in society as a whole, profanity is not considered a common way of communicating. So when we teach and influence our children we must remember that our values and morals must reflect the values and morals of society as a whole, not just what is valued in our own household or neighborhood. Not teaching our children that there is a big world outside of our very own existence is counterproductive to their development. For example, when we teach our children to fight or to defend themselves it's rare that we teach them the circumstance in which this type of behavior is appropriate or even warranted. I don't know if it's just plain ole foolishness or just simple ignorance that makes us not realize that fighting is against the law. I know and understand that it may be common in some households and even a way of life in some neighborhoods, but in the eyes of society, which encompasses more than our own little neighborhoods and communities, it's illegal to strike another individual against their will! I can't tell you how frustrating it is to hear in this time and age that parents are still encouraging their children to hurt others when confronted with a conflict. What kind of Tom Foolery is this? As the adults we should know that most children lack the ability to resolve conflicts without utilizing a rational thought process. So it is our responsibility as parents and even more so as fathers to teach them how to resolve conflicts without physical aggression. The consequences can be far greater than what we anticipate. I'm not condoning the idea of allowing our children to be battered and beaten. But what I'm saying is there's a time and a place for everything depending on the circumstances. Teaching our children to settle disputes with physical aggression in today's society can bring outcomes that may be harmful to the development of our children well into adulthood. And remember, when a child is no longer considered a child but an adult, they are accountable for the choices they make. But as adults we are responsible for teaching, guiding, and influencing their decision-making process as a child. So when we teach our children to settle their disputes with fighting just remember that to choose the act is to choose the consequence. Think about it, battery is punishable by incarceration; injuries may be sustained from fighting and most devastating of all is that people lose their lives every day over settling disputes with violence. If you want to teach your son how to be a man, teach him how to be a better man and model those expectations for him. If you want to teach your daughter how to be a woman, show her how to be a better woman who respects herself and model what a better man should be so that she knows what to expect from men who seek her favor.

It is our responsibility to prepare our children for the world as it really is, not for what we think it should be and for what they want it to be. Providing our children with a false sense of reality does nothing more than place them at a disadvantage when it comes to being prepared for society and the world as it really is. One of the most important things you could give your child has no monetary value, it doesn't have a name brand on it, and it's not tangible. Your time, guidance, and influence transcend all things that are material in nature. We all know things that are tangible become temporary. Therefore, the relationship we build with our children should be built on things that are intangible and eternal. The time you spend with your child teaching them to read, watching and discussing television, conversing about issues in their lives, attending church, and even just hanging out with them will have more of an impact on the type of individual that he or she develops to be much more so than any material item ever will. Material items can never compensate for the lack of effort we put in the development of our children.

For those who strive to be better men, more often than not we fail to get the recognition for being the men that we are. And I know that sometimes this can be discouraging for a lot of us. But our goal is not to receive any awards or recognition. I know it's nice to be appreciated from time to time but we have to learn to encourage ourselves and not look for or expect others to. If we waited for our women and our children or anyone else to commend us we would be disappointed more times than not. Our recognition and our reward should be found in the success of raising productive, respectful, pro-social, educated, and responsible individuals. Just as our rewards lie in how successful we are at raising our children, we must be aware that we bear some responsibility in the unsuccessful development of their character. The role we play in the desired outcome of our children is solely based on our own disposition. While understanding this, we should also understand that we can ultimately make choices that can be viewed as of great consequence in trying to achieve our accomplishments. So when we discuss the legacy we leave behind for not only ourselves but for our children as well, what will yours be? In what sense will your child use the words *Like My Daddy*?

Chapter 4

Excuses

E xcuses. What are they and what do they sound like? Excuses are things people say to cover up the truth. A lot of times people, especially men, use excuses to justify their shortcomings. By no means is not having a father figure in my life an excuse for my shortcomings and I realized that a long time ago. As a matter of fact, I realized it the first time I was faced with a situation I couldn't control. When men feel like they've lost control of whatever the situation is, they tend to immediately look for ways to regain that control. We hardly ever bother to think about why we lost the control in the first place and what steps to take to make sure we don't lose it again. And when I say lose control, I don't mean control over a particular individual—more so a situation or a condition. Men have a common characteristic that reaches across all cultures, races, and ethnicities, and that's the need to be in control, whether it's control of their life, household, or family. More times than not, a lack of control leads to excuses. For example, I'm sure when the day comes that I decide to sit down with my father he'll probably give me plenty of excuses as to why he lived less than ten minutes from me my whole life and never bothered to take responsibility for me. On the other hand, he might just tell me he never gave a damn! Men will make excuses as to why they can't sustain a viable relationship and even why they can't or won't be a father to their children when in reality all the excuses in the world can't cover up the truth, and the truth is that we're not the men our women, children, and families need us to be.

There are many factors that can be attributed to our inability or our unwillingness to meet certain expectations. One of the primary factors is that there are very little to no expectations to meet. For example, as far as relationships are concerned, women have lowered their expectations as to what a man should be and this is partly due to a combination of things such as disappointment, discouragement, desperation, and hopelessness. In some cases even ignorance can be attributed to such low expectations. Of course issues like low self-esteem, insecurities, and poor self-value play vital roles in the lowering of these same expectations as well. Just as it is difficult for a woman to teach a boy how to be a better man, it's even harder for a woman to teach a young woman what a better man is or what a better man should be and what expectations to have. This is partly due to our inability to sustain viable relationships. The majority of African American women are raising their children alone—outside of the commitment of marriage. There is no example of a healthy relationship to model for young women to see and understand so that they know what expectations to set forth in their own relationships. When a young child sees a healthy relationship between a man and a woman, the likelihood of instilling those values and expectations are greater than not. When a daughter or a young girl is shown a male figure who is nurturing, confident, respectful, kind yet strong, and takes responsibility for the lives for which he is responsible, those are some of the same qualities she looks for in her relationship. A good friend of mine once told me that "a woman chooses a man; a man doesn't choose a woman." So as men we are obligated to take responsibility for ourselves as well as the women who choose to allow us to court their favor. If our women lack self-respect, self-esteem, and value for themselves, then we have to accept responsibility for their shortcomings. Just as our women are filled with disappointment, discouragement, desperation, and hopelessness, we have to take ownership for what we've played a part in creating. This concept applies to our women because once again, oftentimes we become the source of their insecurities, low self-esteem, and lack of self-value. Now don't take that statement the wrong way! We can't allow women to use men as an excuse for all of their shortcomings, God forbid! But what we do have to take responsibility for is us. And when I say us I mean the African American community, and it starts with our men. Once we realize that we have to take responsibility for us and not expect anyone else to— i.e., the government, schools, civic organizations, etc.— then expectations become more than expectations; they become the norm and eventually the status quo.

We don't necessarily have to be a part of an organization to create change. We're individual change agents in that we can initiate change at the most crucial point, in our own homes. Each man must make a conscious decision to do the right thing by his woman, child, and family as a whole each and every day. In order for this to happen there has to be some sort of spiritual foundation or connection. For without such a foundation or connection there is no guidance as to what is considered right and what is wrong. Now we all know that we struggle with moral dilemmas every day and I'm not saying that you have to be what I call a "Holy Roller," but what I am saying is that we all know that our morals and values originate from the holy word (the Bible). Therefore it's only natural that we have to have some sort of spiritual foundation or connection in order to know and do what is consciously and morally right. I don't know if that means you have to attend someone's church every Sunday or if the values and morals Grandma taught you are sufficient, but without them we're as blind as Ray Charles sitting in a room with the lights out wearing a pair of dark shades.

So excuses are something we men, and yes I said *we* (just because I'm the author I can't excuse myself from being a man), can't use to cover up the truth and we (there I go using that *we* word again) can't allow excuses to keep us from taking responsibility for us. As I think about my inspirations for this book I reflect on my two younger brothers. Both have been married and one has even divorced. What I admire about them both is their relentless, everlasting, and undying love for their children. The older of my younger brothers divorced after five years of marriage. Contrary to popular opinion, divorce is not necessarily a bad thing. I strongly believe in being happy. Happiness is a necessity of life and anyone who tells you any different has an unnatural perception of what life really is or at least what life should be. People don't generally live to be miserable, they live to be happy. So when my younger brother divorced because of his inability to be happy with his wife, I understood. But what was so surprising was that it made him a better father to his children. He became more nurturing, involved, caring, and is a role model for them. He builds his life around them and has made a conscious decision to ensure that he plays a significant role in their development in becoming better men, fathers, and husbands. To suggest that the presence of these attributes were surprising implies that they were nonexistent initially. For whatever the reasons, the implications may very well have been valid. But whatever the reasons were, they helped transform him into a better man. Notice I didn't say a perfect man or even the best man. Just better than what he was before.

The younger of the two siblings has made an even greater sacrifice and has dedicated himself to raising his daughters in the same manner along with committing himself to a relationship that is forever evolving and is even harder work than his regular nine to five. I don't think either of them realizes how proud I am of them for being the men they are. What's so intriguing yet ironic is that the younger of the two has a son from a previous relationship and, just as my father did, he lives less than ten minutes from him. Yet, he takes responsibility for him by providing financial and emotional support, and has made a conscious decision to play a significant role in his guidance, development, and influence as a better man. I can only hope that I played some small part in influencing and guiding them in becoming the men they are. Now, I'm not saying they're perfect! By no stretch of the imagination! But I am saying that I do admire some of the values and ideals they have in common. In some instances my ideals are viewed as conservative and in some ways they are. For example, my personal views on abortion are that I don't believe in them, but I do believe in the right of a woman to choose her own fate.

Some may view these principles as conventional but I would argue that they're based on taking a realistic view of the big picture. In looking at the big picture, the expectation is that each and every man should be able to take his destiny into his own hands and be responsible for himself. Some self-proclaimed African American intellectuals may disagree with this point of view but theoretically it's consistent with the very tenets of our country. This is why I would contend that we are responsible for us. We have expected others to be responsible for us for so long that we use others as excuses for our shortcomings as men. We blame everyone from the schools and the government to our Caucasian counterparts for our lack of responsibility for ourselves, our relationships, and our families, while at the same time attempting to avoid the consequences of our own choices. And, yes, we do have choices. Many would argue that at times we are left without choices and that the circumstances on which our choices are based have been influenced by external factors beyond our control. As men we've fallen short of being what and who we need to be and there's no one to blame for our choices but ourselves. I know there are several views that would refute this perception but the reality is that if we accept excuses for our shortcomings, then the development that needs to take place will never occur. Excuses are things that should never be considered when we're discussing the plight of our very existence as better men. I apologize in advance for not concurring with the theory that there is a conspiracy by the government and our Caucasian counterparts to make us terrible fathers to our children, horrible husbands to our women, and niggers in general! We do a good job ourselves at creating these images independent of the help of others. I know and understand that not every opportunity has been afforded to us as African Americans but I say where there is no opportunity, create one! It's important to know that we should not expect anyone to give us anything. Theoretically we all know what the world should be like. Unfortunately the world as we know it today is not a utopia. The reality is that the status quo is not going to willingly share in the wealth and success that they've created for the benefit of themselves and their own heirs. And I'm sure there are many who would argue that we as African Americans helped create that wealth and success. Well, I say if we helped create that wealth and success, then we should be able to create it for ourselves, but only if we can keep from impeding upon each other by continuously failing at taking on the responsibility to which we are obligated. I'm not saying that wealth is the key to being a better man, but being successful in setting and achieving goals that are conducive to providing a genuine, sincere care and concern for others is. Excuses are things that hamper our growth and development. So it's understandable to see how there is very little room for excuses in our evolution as men.

When we discuss our progression in becoming better men, sustaining better relationships, and treating our relationships with our women and children, it is inevitable that excuses will play some part in placing responsibility and accountability on anyone or anything other than ourselves. As I said before, excuses are things that people use to cover up the truth. In becoming better men we have to stop using excuses that place blame on outside or external entities. Even more so, we can't let external circumstances dictate who we are. I'm not saying that we can't be flexible and open-minded, but our foundation must remain as the core of our manhood. Once we establish our core principles we're bound by those same ideologies. What we believe to be right and just is just that! That's why establishing those core principles is so important and should be recognized as a focal point in our development. It's unfortunate that I'm fortunate enough to be in a position to make an impact on those I come in contact with on a daily basis. I consider it unfortunate because being in a position to make an impact on others places me in a situation that's disadvantageous in helping those who are genuinely and sincerely seeking guidance and influence. Even so, as I evolve and develop into a better man I recognize the need to guide and influence others who are less conscious than I am. I'm confronted with it day in and day out. I sit across the table from us daily and I ponder the idea of making an impact on the lives of others in some form or fashion. As we attempt to play our role in the scheme of the big picture it becomes difficult and almost impossible when we choose to attempt to compete with others while lacking a basic accredited high school diploma, not being able to pass a simple drug or background screening, and lacking the basic skills to function in society as a whole. I can honestly say that it is truly frustrating to be placed in a position to change the lives of those of us who are complacent with mediocre skills while my concern for us is more than our concerns for ourselves. Oops! Did I say mediocre? I meant substandard or none at all. We all are faced with an opportunity at some point in our lives to make an impact on others in some small way, shape, or form. More often than not we encounter low social skills combined with very low educational skills in our own day-to-day lives. When placed in these types of situations we're often faced with a difficult quandary. The question is do we provide opportunities for those of us who are apparently not qualified, ill-prepared, or ill-equipped to take advantage of these same opportunities just because it's us? Or do we set the expectations and hold us accountable when we don't meet them? This is just one of the dilemmas we're faced with every day and we can't allow excuses to be the deciding factor in justifying our own inadequacies. If so, we're enabling the very same existence that we claim to have grown tired of. So as we encounter us in a state that is less than better, we should and must take responsibility for us and not allow us to let excuses deter us from fulfilling our obligation to us.

I've found that not only as men but as African Americans in particular we're inclined to prefer to take shortcuts, not only in certain aspects of our day-to-day lives but in life in general. In some instances this can be misconstrued as being lazy and in some cases it's exactly what it appears to be. When it comes to certain objectives we tend to make excuses as to why it's okay to utilize shortcuts as a means of reaching those objectives. But as African Americans and especially as better men we must understand that shortcuts should not be considered a way of life. And what I'm discussing is the way we attempt to circumvent the necessary process in order to obtain our desired outcomes. I know we see people of other cultures and backgrounds take shortcuts every day and it's rational to see nothing wrong with it if society allows it. But isn't that what makes us better, the ability to stand aside from the others?

We can see these efforts in an array of instances that we encounter in our day-to-day lives. For example, a lot of times we choose to take shortcuts in obtaining things such as education, employment, wealth, and even relationships. When we choose to take shortcuts in pursuing educational credentials by paying for credentials that lack accreditation or recognition, we deny ourselves the opportunity to obtain quality instruction that is distinguished and recognized as such. Establishments such as these offer the allure of completing a post secondary education faster through eliminating the basic core courses that develop writing and analytical skills necessary to be competent and efficient when competing with others in the workforce. I'm not saying there is anything wrong with attending an institute of this caliber, but we should be aware that if the objective is to build a career, not just get a job, we need to understand that it is necessary to have acceptable writing and communication skills that are usually found in core educational components. A lot of times we use excuses such as "school isn't for everyone" as a justification for the shortcuts we take, rather than taking the more conventional method of obtaining formal credentials. This is just one of the instances in which we use shortcuts as a means of attempting to establish ourselves as equally qualified as other individuals with whom we compete. When in reality we lack the skills necessary to be competitive in an ever changing workforce. The bar is constantly being raised and we're failing to rise to the occasion in many instances. As better men, we can't allow shortcuts to become a part of our character. As far as education is concerned, we do nothing more than defraud ourselves and create a false sense of security.

When it comes to wealth we often take shortcuts in lieu of having a strong work ethic and laboring relentlessly for what we earn. Shortcuts can be seen in how we as men and especially as African American men turn to illegal activities that place not only ourselves but others in jeopardy while creating an unhealthy image for our women and children to witness. Our lethargic nature can even be seen in the way we view employment opportunities. Most often we prefer to seek assistance with employment through favors and handouts rather than gaining employability skills and obtaining gainful employment through our own achievement, not from the assistance of others. Granted, we all know that there are times when certain opportunities present themselves that allow not just us, but others the prospect of gaining employment through networking and partnerships. But others should not be the sole basis of our own employment opportunities. Better men create opportunities for themselves and others by developing employability skills and taking it upon themselves to make an honest effort at seeking and attaining the opportunities to which they aspire.

Believe it or not we even take shortcuts in establishing relationships with others. Not all but most men would prefer to enter into physical relationships sooner than later as opposed to taking the time to establish the physical relationship through spending time together, conversing, and getting to know each other. In these instances taking shortcuts may involve bartering or exchanging material things such as money, gifts, and big-ticket items in an attempt to surpass the process of spending time together, conversing, and getting to know each other in an attempt to gain physical gratification. Now this is not the case in all instances but it's not uncommon for many and is an ordinary practice for some. For many this is a common practice in the development of physical relationships between men and women. As better men our perception of what we should be to our women disallows us to take shortcuts when it comes to our day-to-day expectations of what life is and should be. As better men we know and understand that shortcuts are counterproductive to what we strive to achieve and are not conducive to being better as a whole. Shortcuts are not things we should admire or condone. They should be seen as we see all excuses, things people use to cover up the truth.

When it comes to making excuses for our relationships we can no longer point the finger at our better halves. Some might ask, Why not? We can no longer place the blame on others because if we strive to be better men, that means not only taking responsibility for us, it also means being a better man and taking responsibility for our relationships. I've always believed that it's much easier to take the safe way out and place blame on the opposite side of the spectrum, but it takes a better man to take responsibility for his part in an unsuccessful relationship. Please don't interpret this as meaning men are responsible for all of our failed relationships. Women can be equally as responsible as men in placing blame on failed relationships.

When I thought I had found a union made in heaven, my best friend and soul mate, I thought there wasn't anything we couldn't accomplish together. When this perfect union expired, a good friend of mine told me that she would find me a Hispanic woman because she would appreciate me more. I never bothered to tell her that regardless of how or why my relationship ended, I would never allow it to be an excuse for me to change who I am and seek comfort from a woman outside of my box or preference. Of course this is why it's essential in understanding the importance of who we choose to deal with when it comes to relationships. Remember that there are consequences when it comes to love and relationships. So there are things to consider when we choose to deal with individuals, whether it's on a casual or formal basis. Things we should bear in mind are: is this individual someone I would want as the mother of my child if she unintentionally or intentionally gets pregnant? Is this someone I would want to be obligated to in order to be the man I need to be for my child? Is she inside or outside of my box and am I willing to settle for less than what I expect? With all of these questions taken into account, an assessment of what's most important should be reflected upon. But more than that, as men we must first find value in the aspect of attaining a sustainable relationship. It's understandable that coming to this revelation is not an easy task as the idea of having several different women at one time can be very tempting. Even so, the strength, love, and support of one woman can satisfy the desire for many. So excuses become irrelevant when compared to what is considered to be a viable relationship.

One of the most important aspects of being a better man is the ability to cultivate a relationship in an attempt to establish a foundation for growth and development. So while we point the finger and lay blame, we must ask ourselves what role we played in the unsuccessful attempt at establishing a workable relationship. Explanations such as *she didn't have herself together* or *she has too much baggage* are things we say to cover up the truth. If she doesn't have herself together, then help her get it together. Be the man she needs you to be. Be that leader, protector, teacher, and head of household. If she has too much baggage, then help her with her baggage and carry the load. Women are not only the weaker sex physically but it can also be said that they are much weaker emotionally. So whatever baggage they carry, whether it's physical or emotional, we as men should be able to help carry the load. Be the man she needs you to be. What is most difficult in being a better man is being able to sacrifice our own insecurities when resolving issues in our relationships. A lot of times we allow our egos and insecurities to play a part in our own inability to take responsibility for our relationships, not only as better men but as men in general. We allow these things to become rationalizations for our lack of forgiveness in accepting the shortcomings of our potential mate or partner. The excuses we use to cover up the truth do nothing more than enable us to justify our own shortcomings as men. This is why I contend that our own male egos create stubbornness and inflexibility in resolving relevant issues in our relationships with our female counterparts. This is one of the most significant issues when it comes to developing meaningful relationships with our wives, girlfriends, and casual partners. So we can't allow our egos to continue to be used as excuses in how we approach relationships and the idea of being a better man as it pertains to the way we relate to our counterparts. The reason why excuses are intolerable in relationships is because as men it is our place to lead, and if we don't understand that as men, and women don't understand that as women, then we'll continue to have difficulties in establishing and maintaining viable relationships. I understand how difficult it is gaining the confidence of our female counterparts who have been disappointed time and time again. But that statement alone sounds all too familiar. As a matter of fact, it sounds a lot like an excuse! Remember, it's not our goal to control them by exploiting their emotions and insecurities. It is our intent to utilize those emotions and insecurities to create tools and to guide and to help them, not hurt them. That's how you earn the respect of being a better man. Be that as it may, it is necessary we understand that the things beyond our control are less relevant when it comes to making excuses for our relationships. Being better in our relationships leaves very little room for excuses and being better has to be our overall intent. So as we contemplate the shortcomings of our relationships, excuses become significant barriers to the growth and maturation of what is expected. We should always make attempts to encourage our better halves rather than discourage them. These are all the things we should want for ourselves and our relationships with our women. These are the things that are essential to the development of what is considered to be a functional relationship, which in turn sets the foundation for a functional and loving family. The expectations have to be set before we can attain them. So we have to do more than what we've been doing; we have to give more than what we've been giving. In other words, when we think we've done enough and we think we've given enough, do more and give more!

As we discuss not only the desire but the necessity to be better fathers to our children, excuses are things that become barriers to the development of productive relationships with our children. We tend to use excuses to justify our lack of responsibility for our own indiscretions and by indiscretions I mean our inability to make good decisions when it comes to the circumstances in which our children are conceived. For those who have thought through their decision to raise children and who to raise them with, this particular statement does not apply. But for those it does apply to, we have to make better choices of why, when, and with whom we choose to conceive our children. Like I previously stated, it's understood that every relationship does not necessarily mean that the intent is to conceive children but only to fulfill a physical want or need. But as stated before, with relationships and love come consequences and the same can be said for the excuses we employ as barriers or hurdles to change. Excuses for the consequences of our actions are by no means a rationalization for our lack of obligation to our children. We could easily say that a failed relationship or the lack thereof is reason enough to excuse a lack of responsibility or obligation to what is ultimately considered to be our legacy. The excuse of being too young or ill-prepared to be a father has little to no validity when it comes to taking responsibility for what we create. It is typical for these types of excuses to become things we use to cover up the truth. Making excuses for little things like not seeing your child for days to weeks or even months at a time does not negate your responsibility for them. A simple phone call can suffice for a lack of daily physical interaction. Making excuses for not establishing a line of communication with your children does not pardon your inability to establish a productive relationship with them. Just as we can't allow excuses to justify our inability or unwillingness to be better fathers to our children, we can't allow our children to make excuses as to why they can't or won't live up to their responsibilities in the relationship. And yes, children bear responsibilities in relationships as well as we do. We can't allow them to be irresponsible when it comes to the father and child relationship just because we are the adults. Children have obligations just as adults do. The difference is that their responsibilities are set by the adult. If norms and expectations are not set by the father or any adult for that matter, then the norms and expectations will be set by the child. So if we don't expect our children to want to be better than what they are, then they'll never be. If we don't expect our children to be responsible for understanding their role in the parent/child relationship or even the adult/child relationship then children tend to create what they think the relationship should be. So excuses are things that are intolerable when we're discussing the relationships we create as fathers. The truth is that as men we have lacked the sense of obligation to our children regardless of the circumstances in which we create them or in which they are born. It doesn't matter that you're too young, it doesn't matter that it was a one-night stand, it doesn't matter if you don't love her, it doesn't even matter that you don't have a job. What matters is that you are obligated to be the provider, teacher, protector, and head of the household for whom you are responsible. The absence of our presence as men and as fathers in the lives of our children is demoralizing enough without alluding to the fact that the mere absence of our presence creates guilt, shame, and embarrassment. A lot of times we tend to allow that same guilt, shame, and embarrassment to keep us from establishing viable relationships with our children. The existence of these very undesirable feelings does not negate our roles and responsibilities as fathers. When it comes to being a better man and in turn a better father, excuses such as being absent in the life of your child are objectionable when considering the establishment of a viable relationship. Even so, there are factors to consider when approaching such a task. One should take into consideration that along with the absence of your presence is the absence of a foundation from which to work, so the establishment of a foundation should be well thought out. Not only should it be well thought out, it should be solicited first and foremost. Not every child will be receptive to the establishment of a relationship with someone who has been considered as nonexistent. It's difficult to gain the understanding and trust of someone who may have had feelings of resentment and discontent. As men and fathers we should understand that these types of feelings are common among children who have been denied the privilege, and yes, once again it's a privilege to have the love, guidance, and influence of a father figure. We should also notice that I used the word "difficult" and not "impossible." With all of the resentment, discontent, and disdain, if the intent is to establish something that is or has been lacking, then the aforementioned obstacles are surmountable. So we should cease in allowing excuses to be the things we use to cover up the truth. The truth is that we've failed in being the fathers we need to be to our children, regardless of the circumstances in which we've created them. Be that as it may, the reality is that when the opportunity presents itself, what are we prepared to do to make what was wrong right again?

Let's be mindful of this: my insight is not based on some big scientific hypothesis or theory. My perspective is based on real-world experiences. Albeit, not every experience is the same; we can all agree that experience carries a smaller burden of proof than that of any theory or hypothesis. So as we digest the premise of becoming a better man let's not only consider the content of the idea, let's ponder the source of the concept. There are some who would argue that research and data are necessary in order to provide a more accurate account for some of the points that have been raised in this piece. What is being presented are issues and situations that are realistic and concrete. These are issues that each and every one of us can relate to on a daily basis. So as we become enlightened and maybe even intrigued by the subject matter, let's ensure that our focus remains with us and not with those who choose to be pessimistic and discouraging. Remember, the focus of _**"And We Call Ourselves Men!"**_ remains with us and how we can and should take responsibility for us in becoming better men. It's understood that there are and will be injustices of the world and we should definitely recognize them and resolve them at every opportunity in which they arise. But we also have to decide if we're going to be a part of the problem or a part of the solution. Remember, we all have a choice in the decisions we make. For those of us who choose to be a part of the problem I say: stand aside and let those of us that can lead, lead. And for those of us who choose to be a part of the solution I say: Do more! Do more for yourself, do more for your relationships, do more for your children, and do more for your family and others. In the end we all have to look at ourselves in the mirror and ask ourselves, *what have I gotten done?* Well, in my 38 years of existence I've completed two college degrees, while working on a third. I've traveled the world while in the military to include living in Europe for two years. I've made some good decisions and I've made some bad. I've developed and created a mentoring program that has targeted at-risk youth. I've seen some of those very same at-risk youth become better than what they were before I met them. I've even had a few find me and tell me that they would have never made it out of high school if it wasn't for my guidance and influence. I've had men tell me that I'm a better man than they are because of my conviction in being just that, better. I've attempted to put myself in a position that allows me to provide guidance and influence to others by taking on a leadership role in my life, my relationships, and as a role model for others. I've put myself in a position to provide others with opportunities that may not have been afforded to them otherwise. I continue to seek improvement in things I know I struggle with so that I may make myself a better man. I'm definitely not what some would consider to be rich or famous and some have even gone as far as to say that I'm already a better man. But I think I've yet to accomplish what I and so many like me strive every day to be. I've yet to reach the pinnacle of my potential. And at the date of this release, I'll be a published author. So am I perfect? Of course not! My legacy may be determined by to what extent I'm able to guide and influence others with a genuine and sincere care and concern. But I try to be better than what is expected of me. I try to exceed what society perceives me to be. I'm conscious of it and I make an effort time and time again regardless of the circumstances I have no control over. It is not my intent to achieve fame and fortune, nor is it my intent to attain power and influence. Neither of these two objectives is a prerequisite for being a better man. I understand that having fame and fortune along with power and influence is not a necessity for self-growth or making an impact on others. For having these attributes does not a better man make. Most of all, I've made a conscious attempt to be a better man than my father is and was to me. I once thought that I would never have anything to thank him for because of his nonexistent presence in my life. But in retrospect, his absence has contributed to much of the success I've enjoyed over my lifetime. Ironically his absence has illustrated to me exactly what a better man should be and that is the precise opposite of him. With that being said, I think I've accomplished several things in my life but I think, no, I know I could have accomplished so much more if I would have had the guidance and influence necessary for all of us as men and especially African American men to be better in taking responsibility for not only ourselves but for those we are accountable for also. There are some who may consider my accomplishments insignificant and there are even some who may say I think I know it all. But like so many others, I've overcome the odds, I've exceeded expectations, and I've risen above the statistics. So in my eyes that makes my accomplishments very relevant. The relevance of my accomplishments is that they make me better. I'm not necessarily speaking in the sense of being better than others, but better than what I was or what statistics say I should be. So when I look in the mirror I ask myself every day, w*hat's next: which expectations do*

I exceed next, which odds do I overcome and which statis-tics do I rise above next? These are the questions that we should all be eager to answer. And for those who may think of me as a "Mr. Know-it-all" I say this: It is neither my claim nor my intent to know it all. However, there are some things I do know and that is if we continue to turn the ta-bles on placing the responsibility and the accountability for making us better, then we will continue to struggle with the role we play in the development and achievement of us and the outcome will remain ineffectual.

In keeping all of this in mind, I've had to find my own way through life mainly because there was no one there to take responsibility for my development as a better man. So like I previously stated, excuses are things people use to cover up the truth. I have no excuse for my failures or dis-appointments, nor do I seek them. The truth is that if I falter or if I fail at being better, it's not because my father wasn't there or because someone else didn't do what I should have been responsible for. It's because of the decisions I chose to make, nothing more and nothing less. So once again, am I perfect? And once again I say of course not! Now ask yourself what have you gotten done? What have you done to make yourself a better man, son, brother, husband, or father? What is your legacy and what will you be remem-bered for? What's next for you? These are the questions we should all ask ourselves day in and day out. The answers you provide yourself with should be the catalyst you use to take responsibility for yourself and us! *And we call our-selves men?* Then and only then will we be able to call our-selves men.